Also by Brigitte van Tuijl

Ontdek Wat Je Écht Wilt En Maak Daar (Je) Werk Van
The Gap - bridge the space between where
you are and where you want to be

The Art of Divine Selfishness Series
Book One: Unmute Your Life - break free from
fear & go for what you REALLY want

The Art of Divine Selfishness

TRANSFORM YOUR LIFE, YOUR BUSINESS & THE WORLD BY PUTTING YOU FIRST.

BOOK 2 IN THE 'THE ART OF DIVINE SELFISHNESS' SERIES

BRIGITTE VAN TUIJL

ISBN Paperback: 978-90-830654-4-1
ISBN e-book: 978-90-830654-5-8
Visit www.booksbybrigitte.com for more books by the author
For additional gifts, visit www.selfishbookgift.com

The information provided in this book is designed to inspire, educate, motivate, and enlighten you on the subjects discussed. It's not meant as a substitute for professional coaching or other expert assistance. If such level of assistance is required, please seek the services of a competent professional or contact the author directly for one-to-one coaching options. The author assumes no liability for use of the information and exercises.

Copy editor: Kelly Urgan
Cover design: Susan D. Johnson
Interior Design by FormattedBooks.com

Contents

Part 2 — Questions, Fears, Concerns

Introduction

In the past twenty years of coaching women, I noticed that several themes were *always* part of our work together. Being true to yourself and your dreams regardless of what others think. Doing your own thing and honoring what's right for you, even when others disapprove. Prioritizing your dreams, yourself, and your self-care, instead of putting yourself aside for others (or your to-do list) at your own detriment.

Honoring yourself and your desires—let alone putting yourself first!—is something most women find tricky. They're afraid to be criticized and no longer be liked. They're afraid of their power and often put other people's needs before their own. This leaves them feeling tired and longing for more freedom at best, and resentful, angry, and burned out at worst.

The reason this is an issue for most women is because women have been silenced, marginalized, and suppressed for centuries. (And today we're still not being treated as equals in all areas of our society, let alone in all countries on the planet!) This has left its mark on all women. We learned to fear our power, dim our light, tone down our personalities and make ourselves smaller. This hurts our sense of freedom and every other area of our life. From the outside it may seem like this doesn't bother many women. They have a wonderful life and career. But that doesn't mean they feel happy, free, or fulfilled. It doesn't mean they don't worry about being liked. And it doesn't mean they have enough time for themselves.

I think it's about time this changes. There's no need to burn yourself up trying to be someone you're not. It's absolutely possible to create a business and life that brings you more freedom, fulfillment, happiness, and joy—*without* feeling guilty, changing who you are, doing things you hate or wearing yourself out. On the contrary, you can achieve these things by being MORE true to yourself, and by honoring yourself, your needs, and your dreams *more than ever before*!

You become more yourself by letting go of expectations you don't want to live up to. By no longer changing who you are to fit in. By no longer toning down your true self, your zest for life, your potential for success, or your well-being or joy.

This book helps you achieve that. It shows you how to let go of behaviors that no longer serve you. It helps you see yourself for who you truly are and how to be even more true to yourself. You learn how to release feelings of guilt and the fear of making waves. You connect with yourself and your desires on a much deeper level. And you learn how to act on this deeper connection as well!

When you do this, you become what I call Divinely Selfish: you put yourself, your *soul*, first. As a result, you gain more freedom, happiness, well-being, and joy. You feel more powerful and energized. You benefit when you become Divinely Selfish. So do your business, your life, people around you, and even the world!

In the following chapters I explain what Divine Selfishness is, and how it's different from regular selfishness (which is NOT what I promote). We dive deeper into the downsides of *not* being Divinely Selfish. I also explain how *everyone* benefits when you put yourself first, and I share how I learned to be Divinely Selfish.

Then, I take you on a journey that shows you how you, too, can put yourself, your needs, your dreams, and desires first. So you transform in the best ways—and the people and the world around you can benefit from your transformation.

Get ready for more inner freedom, power, and joy. For more time for yourself and less stressing over things you're not responsible for.

You're about to go through a metamorphosis and are in for a liberating ride. Buckle up and enjoy!

To being Divinely Selfish,

so you can serve without suffering,

and feel happy, free, and fulfilled.

Love,

Brigitte

What is Divine Selfishness?!

This is the second book in The Art of Divine Selfishness series. So, what exactly is Divine Selfishness, and how does this book fit in?

Divine Selfishness means to put your soul first. To live the life your soul chose to experience. To live YOUR life, instead of a life others want, or expect, you to live. To do that, you need to put yourself first: your needs, wants, desires, and your truth, which is, of course, the selfish part of Divine Selfishness. The Divine part has to do with the fact that you put your *soul* first. You come from your *heart*. When you do this, you automatically contribute to the well-being of all.

The universe doesn't make mistakes. Every living being has a place and a purpose, which is ALWAYS to contribute to the whole. When you put your soul first, when you put *yourself* first, you automatically serve others. You serve others by being who you truly are and doing what you most love! Just like bees and bananas have their place in the unity that is life and contribute to it by simply being who they are.

Being Divinely Selfish means you can serve without suffering, without changing who you are, without doing things you hate. Being Divinely Selfish is quite the contrary! You follow your joy, your heart, the path your soul lays out for you.

This differs vastly from the selfishness that comes from fear, lack, neediness, or greed. Shallow self-centeredness serves only one person: you. Selfishness is disconnected from the heart, from the soul, from love. But Divine Selfishness? Serves all.

You can, of course, only do what you love when (a) you know what you want—what you REALLY want, and (b) you honor it. That's why the first book in this series, *Unmute Your Life - break free from fear & go for what you REALLY want*, focused purely on those two topics.

Once you know what you truly want, you still need practical skills and tools to help you put yourself first, such as saying NO, setting boundaries, and more. That's where this book comes in. It helps you liberate yourself from habits, beliefs, and behaviors that no longer serve you and make you feel unfulfilled, unhappy, and unfree. Learning to be Divinely Selfish fulfills you, and helps you serve others at a higher level, too!

The Downside of Not Being Divinely Selfish

When you don't put yourself first, it's easy to get overworked and feel tired. You lose energy and don't have enough time for yourself. You often feel you don't get enough in return from the effort you put in and you can start to feel resentful.

You can feel unfulfilled and unhappy. Trapped in a cage. There's so much more you want out of life. You sometimes feel you've lost parts of yourself. You don't always speak your mind and make yourself smaller. It doesn't feel good. But you're not sure how to change that. And that annoys you even more.

You're always there for others, but you don't have enough time for things that matter to you.

Your life feels muted. You often feel you want to express more, be more, *live* more—but how?

At best, you'll feel tired and unfulfilled. At worst, you will burn out.

All these feelings negatively impact your business, too! You work too hard. Your business doesn't bring you the freedom you crave. Your clients are happy, but you? Not as much as you'd like. You compromise on things that matter to you, and you settle for less than you want. You feel you have to sacrifice in order to grow your business. You don't want that, but isn't that part of the deal? You'd like to do things differently, but aren't sure if that's possible. You'd like to be more true to yourself in your business and do things your way, on your terms. You're not doing (enough of) that now.

I could come up with more downsides of not being Divinely Selfish, but you get the picture. And the whole idea of becoming *more* Divinely Selfish already speaks to you anyway or you'd never have picked up this book. It may feel uncomfortable to put yourself first, and it requires some skills you may need to practice. These are all addressed in this book. But before you dive into that, I'd like to remind you of these simple truths: your only purpose in life is to be you. All of you. The REAL you. A soul having a human experience, with a personality, gifts, and character traits unique to you and your path.

You contribute the most by being true to yourself. You're happiest and most fulfilled by being true to yourself. In fact, that's all you have to do: to be true to YOU in everything you do.

You were *born* to be you. You can't fail at it. All you have to do is unlearn some things that got in your way. And with everything you do to honor your soul, you get closer to yourself. You come home to *you*.

Welcome home.

How Being Divinely Selfish Transforms Your Life, Your Business, & the World

Being Divinely Selfish changes everything. And it doesn't just serve you—it serves others, too!

How being Divinely Selfish transforms your life

When you put your soul first and are true to who you really are, you automatically live your soul's purpose. You don't have to search for it. All you have to do is honor what you're naturally drawn to do and your purpose unfolds by itself.

Being true to yourself and following your soul brings meaning and fulfillment. It's what makes you happy AND serves others, too.

Being Divinely Selfish enhances your power and makes you feel freer. It energizes you and makes you feel in control of your life. It helps you grow and eliminates intolerable things and energy drains from your life. It brings out your courage and strength.

When you're true to yourself and your soul, you live the life you're supposed to live: YOUR life. The life your soul wants to experience—instead of a life others want you to live.

How being Divinely Selfish serves your business and your clients

By honoring yourself, you get rid of intolerable things in your business, too. You say *yes* to what makes your heart sing and *no* to what doesn't. As a result, your business model will mold itself around you instead of the other way around. Products and services you no longer love will fall away and will be replaced by offers you adore. Because you now love what you do, the quality of your work skyrockets. You're more efficient. Your work no longer drains you and you have more to give. Your clients directly benefit from that!

How your family and friends benefit from you being Divinely Selfish

If you're happier and more energized, that positively affects your family and friends as well! You have more to give to the people you love. You're more fun to be around. You're less snappy, angry, or moody. You're less tired and less stressed.

You model how to take care of yourself and honor your dreams. You also model how to be true to yourself and how you can be a good partner, parent, or friend without draining yourself or selling yourself short. This is beautiful inspiration and an unspoken invitation for people around you to honor *their* souls, aspirations, and dreams more often, too.

How the world benefits

Every living being is part of a greater plan, of life itself. And every living being has a purpose that contributes to others and serves the whole. All you have to do to make that contribution and serve others is to be true to yourself and put your soul first. That's when you do the thing(s) you're born to do. These are the things you love to do. These are the things that serve others and make you happy. It all fits seamlessly together . . . .

When you live your soul's purpose and are true to who you really are, you fulfill the part you came to play in this life. You share the gifts you're born to share.

It doesn't matter what your purpose is or how *big* or *small* it seems: who you are and what you do makes a difference. It matters. Whether it changes the lives of two or of two million people, it's equally important.

You're meant to be exactly who you are and you serve at your highest level by being true to you—the *real* you. The *you* that you were born to be. Your original self. The *you* that you were before you could walk or talk.

All you have to do in this life to be happy AND make a positive difference in the lives of others is to be true to YOU in everything you do. Being Divinely Selfish is how you do that.

How I Learned to Be Divinely Selfish

Growing up, I always felt I wasn't free enough and hated following rules and fulfilling obligations I didn't agree with. I vowed I'd grow up to be completely free and create a life for myself where no one had any say over me.

The primary reason I felt this way was because I was an extreme introvert in an extroverted world. Being introverted doesn't mean you're shy or antisocial. It means you need to be alone to recharge and being around people quickly drains your energy.

Having to go to school five days a week and having family visits every Sunday didn't leave me enough time to be by myself.

School became university and then a job. Family visits were replaced with invitations to parties or other social outings. Which I sometimes enjoy . . . but only when I have enough alone time to balance it out. Which I didn't.

And so I learned to say no and became a pro at setting boundaries and sticking to them. I did my own thing as much as I could and learned to stop caring so much about what others thought about me. I learned to pick friends who loved me for who I was and who didn't try to change me.

By the time I started my business, my personal life was completely introvert-friendly. I designed my life in a way that gave me all the alone time I needed, and I found a good balance between human interaction and being by myself. In my business, it took me some time to find a good balance there, too. (I'll write more about that in one of my upcoming books, *The Happy Hermit - how to thrive as an introvert entrepreneur*.)

You may not be an introvert like me. But I bet there are areas in your business and life where you'd like to feel more free. Areas where you'd like to stop compromising and be true to yourself and your own way of doing things. I bet you'd love to follow your own path without worrying what others think about it. And I bet you'd like to spend more time for yourself in whatever way YOU choose, too!

It might feel impossible to make this happen. It might also feel uncomfortable and scary.

I address your questions and concerns in this book. I know what they are because I lived through them myself and coached countless women on the same issues over the past two decades.

Keep reading and before you know it, you'll be a Divinely Selfish Queen, too! You will greatly benefit. And as I shared in the previous chapter: everyone else will, too!

PART ONE

The Habits, Tips, and Mindset You Need to Become Divinely Selfish

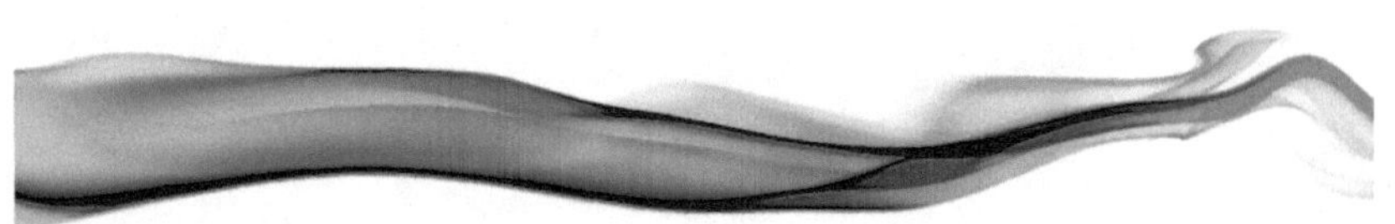

Introduction to Part One

Putting yourself first is easier said than done. It requires skills and habits you never learned or that were frowned upon. And putting your *soul* first? That sounds pretty vague. How can you do *that*? The following chapters show you. Not only how to put your soul first but also how to prioritize yourself, your dreams, your well-being and your needs.

This first part of the book addresses different habits, tips, and mindsets to help you become Divinely Selfish. Every chapter also gives you journal questions to reflect and take action on.

Read through all chapters or simply pick the topics that speak to you.

However you use this book: enjoy!

Chapter 1

Give Yourself Permission

All my clients ask me the same questions.

- "Can I really do that?"
- "Is it okay to make this decision?"
- "Is it okay to say *yes* to this?"
- "Is it okay to say *no* to that?"
- "Can I really do this *my* way?"

I always give them the same answers. Yes, it's really okay. Yes, you can do it *your* way. But it's not *my* permission you need—it's yours.

The same is true for you. Yes, it can help to hear that it's okay to think of yourself more, to say no more, to prioritize your well-being and forge your own path, regardless of what others think of you. It helps to hear that you can be who you are without toning down your opinions or personality. It helps to know that you can do business in your own way, even when no one understands it or approves of it. But if *you* don't give yourself permission to do what you want and be true to yourself, you'll never be able to honor yourself and your desires.

Giving myself permission to *completely* build my business around my desire to spend about 90% of my time alone was the first step to make my business as introvert-friendly as my personal life already was. Other steps were necessary after that, but it began with this important step. (You can read about the rest of the steps in my upcoming book *The Happy Hermit - how to thrive as an introvert entrepreneur.*)

I grant you permission to be YOU and be true to yourself in every area of your business and life. Now all you have to do is give yourself permission, too.

Can you give yourself permission to be all that you are and live and do business accordingly?

If you feel a hint of hesitation, why is that?

Why would it NOT be okay to be you and put your well-being and soul first?

When you ask yourself these questions, you'll find that the answers are echoes of messages you received growing up. Some of these still help you. Others . . . not so much.

ANY message or belief that says you can't be who you are or you can't do what you love is untrue. *UNLESS* what you love most is being a serial killer or torturing small animals. But assuming you don't have these desires, nothing can go wrong when you do what you genuinely love. What you truly love comes straight from your soul. Your deepest joy comes straight from your soul. And when you act in alignment with your soul, you automatically act for the greater good of all. Because at the level of the soul, we're all one and there's only love.

Reflection

If you granted yourself FULL permission to be true to yourself and trusted it was safe to be who you really are, what would you change in your business and personal life?

Divinely Selfish Declarations

* The best person I can be is who I naturally am.
* My purpose in life is to be who I was born to be.
* I give myself full permission to be true to my soul, to my joy, to my desires, and to my needs in every area of my business and life.
* I don't need anyone's permission but my own to be who I am or to walk my own path.

At www.selfishbookgift.com you can get a free permission slip to hang on your wall so you can see it every day (plus some other cool bonuses).

<h1 style="text-align:center">Chapter 2</h1>

<h1 style="text-align:center">Put Your Soul First</h1>

Putting your soul first starts with the decision to say YES to your soul. You can make that decision now, by saying this out loud or writing it down: *I say YES to my soul now. I honor my soul, put her first, listen to her wisdom and guidance, and act on that, too!*

I made that decision when I was thirty and felt stuck in one dead-end job after another. I desperately ached for work that felt meaningful and fulfilling. I had no idea what that could be or how I could find it. So I decided to let my soul show me the way. I don't know what to do next, so I need you to help me out here, I thought. Give me directions and I'll follow them, because I'm DONE doing work that drains me! My soul gave me directions and I listened. Her guidance brought me to a career coach who helped me get clear on my soul's purpose. I continued to follow my soul's guidance and always put her first. This helped me start my business and helped me design a business and life I deeply love.

Your soul gives you directions, too. She speaks to you in dreams, through your intuition, feelings, and emotions. She speaks to you through your joy. She speaks to you in nudges and insights, symbols, and synchronicities, and through that deep-down feeling that tells you what's true for you. If your intuition speaks, it's your soul talking to you.

All you need to do to follow your soul is to listen to your intuition and follow your inner compass. Pay attention to what you KNOW, deep down, and follow that as often as you can.

Asking yourself the following questions can bring you wisdom and answers from your soul, too. Pick the one(s) that resonate with you and act on the answers that come up.

- What would be best for me right now?
- What message does my soul have for me?
- What wants to be done / created / expressed by me today?
- How can I add value to the lives of others today?
- How can I make a positive difference today?
- How can I be an instrument for good today?
- How can I serve others and myself at my highest level today?
- What will bring me joy today?

When you listen to your soul, your actions automatically contribute to the greater good of all. You're part of the universe and connected to everything and everyone. So when you do what's *genuinely* best for you, this benefits others as well.

Reflection

If you put your soul first, what would you do today?

Divinely Selfish Declarations

* I put myself, my soul, first!
* All the happiness, joy, love, and fulfillment I seek come to me as a result of following my soul's guidance.
* My soul knows my path and what's best for me. All I have to do is say yes to the nudges, ideas, and insights she brings me.
* My number one priority is my connection with my soul and putting her first.

Chapter 3

Embrace and Accept All of Who You Are

The main reason it can be hard for you to be true to yourself is because you don't embrace or accept every part of yourself.

That's quite common, so don't beat yourself up if you need some work in this area. I've never met anyone who *fully* accepts and embraces *every* part of herself. No one. Myself included. We all have things we're not proud of, don't want others to know about, or feel ashamed or guilty about.

It's not your fault. We all grew up in a world that tells us how to be and what's expected of us.

You experienced situations where you were shamed for who you were or for something you did or believed. You've been told to take it down a notch or to speak up more. You've been silenced when you wanted to talk, been told to sit down when you wanted to run, and had to obey rules you didn't agree with.

You've been told who you should be and how you should act. You still hear that today! You continue to receive messages about what's done and not done, what's right and what's wrong. The messages differ depending on which circles you run in, but the underlying theme is the same: that you should change something about yourself. That you can't just be *you*, because who you are and what you do is not (good) enough. The message "If you want to be a successful entrepreneur, or be a good parent, or successfully fulfill whatever roles exist in your life, you need to be like this and do like that..." makes it clear how you're *not* supposed to be and what you're *not* supposed to do. These messages make you feel that you're not good enough and you need to change something about you. They make you play smaller and tone yourself down.

The part of me that was always criticized was my introverted side. I've been repeatedly told to be less quiet and to not always say no when someone invited me over. I've often been told I was antisocial or wrong for needing so much alone time. And when I started my business, people kept telling me I needed to network and "get out there!" more. As a result I started to believe I had to change parts of myself if I wanted to build a successful business. Thank god I came to my senses and realized the ONLY way to grow my business AND feel happy was to STOP trying to change myself and to be true to ALL that I am instead.

Maybe you're already aware of the parts of yourself you don't fully accept. If not, answering the following questions will uncover them.

- Is there something about yourself you're not pleased with, something you're ashamed of? Do you think something is wrong about you?
- What if you accepted it? You may not like it or you may have second thoughts about it, but can you acknowledge that it is part of you?
- What if whatever you don't like about yourself is actually your greatest gift? What if it adds value or benefits others? What if this part of you is what makes you unique, makes you *you*, and helps you do whatever you're born to do in this world?

Notice what comes up when you read through these questions. Write it down. If any emotions come up, *feel* them. Let them out in whatever way they come. Maybe you feel sadness, anger, or grief.

That's okay. Let it out. That's part of healing, so don't suppress any of it.

Finally, rewrite your story. Write yourself a love letter. Tell yourself you now accept *all* of who you are, warts and all. *Declare* it. Make it your intention to fully accept and embrace every part of you. You may not instantly feel it. But you'll get there. This is the start. Whatever healing you may still need will come to you at the perfect time.

Reflection

If you fully loved and accepted yourself and knew and trusted it was safe to be you, what would you change in your business and personal life?

Divinely Selfish Declarations

* Who I was born to be is exactly who I'm supposed to be.
* I now fully accept and embrace all that I am.
* I'm already whole.
* I'm good enough.
* I don't have to change a single thing about my true self.
* Who I was born to be is all I need to be.
* All I have to do in this life is to be ME.

Chapter 4

Cut Out the Intolerable

Putting yourself first includes taking good care of yourself. This also means allowing yourself to get the best out of everything. Things you tolerate cost you a lot of energy. With everything you tolerate, you give yourself the message that nothing better is available for you.

Some tolerations are minor annoyances. Others are massive energy drains. But you don't have to put up with ANY of them. You can either stop tolerating what you don't like and create something new or you can change your attitude toward it.

Settling for things (or people!) that aren't ideal for you diminishes your joy. And the more you put up with, the worse you feel about yourself, your life, and what's possible for you.

Cutting out tolerations is something you should regularly check on. Start by making a list now. Once your list is complete, you can cut each item from your list, one at a time.

What are you currently tolerating? Think about all areas of your life and things such as,

- how people treat you,
- toxic relationships,
- clients that don't pay on time,
- itchy pants,
- a leaky faucet,

- uncomfortable shoes, and
- a bad habit.

You *know* when you're settling. How? Because it annoys you every time you're confronted with it. But you do nothing about it. Until now. :-) Let people know which behavior(s) you no longer tolerate. Break up with people who are bad for you. Inform your clients about your new payment policy—and stick to it. Ditch those itchy pants, fix your faucet, and throw out those uncomfortable shoes. Break that habit and hold yourself accountable.

If there's something on your list you can't cut yet, change your attitude toward it. Stop resisting it. Find a perspective on how this serves you, for example. Or make a plan on how you can delete it from your life at a later stage.

You don't have to put up with anything that's bad for you. You never have to tolerate *anything*. YOU hold the key to deal with it. You're not powerless. On the contrary! It's all in your hands.

You may need to gather some courage to stop settling. But you *can* do it! Besides, a lot of tolerations are easy to deal with. All it takes is a firm decision and to take whatever action is needed.

I've tolerated a lot over the years. It took me a while to fire one of my assistants several years ago, for example. I really liked her and didn't want to hurt her feelings. I also feared it would be difficult to find someone better. So I kept working with her. Until I hired someone new for some additional tasks. When I saw how good this new assistant was (and how much more affordable), I finally decided to let my other assistant go. Turned out it wasn't as difficult as I feared it would be. And it freed up so much energy!

That's when I promised myself to settle only for the best from now on. Letting go of things (or people) that aren't the best for you anymore sometimes takes courage in the short run, but you gain so much in the long run that it's always worth it. Life is too short and too precious to settle for anything that doesn't bring you joy!

Reflection

If you stopped settling for less than what you truly want, what would you let go of or change now?

Divinely Selfish Declarations

* I have the power to change everything. I can either change my situation or I can change my attitude toward it.
* I'm more powerful than I think.
* I deserve to be treated with love and respect.
* I don't have to put up with someone else's crap or lousy behavior.
* I'm allowed to receive the best of everything!

Chapter 5

Connect with YOURSELF First

Women can be so busy caring for others, thinking for others, or pleasing others that they (partially) lose their connection with themselves. This leaves you feeling drained and makes it hard to speak out, set boundaries, or communicate your needs. You can't deeply bond with others, either. Your connection with others can only be as deep as your connection with yourself.

The best way to connect with yourself is to be present in this moment, in your body. Be grounded and come from your heart. Tune into your inner world AND to what goes on around you, so you're open, you're present, and you're connected with others.

Getting present in your body and this moment

Use your breath to center yourself—to inhabit your body fully. Breathing in and out deeply and slowly helps with this. Breathe deep into your belly. You can put a hand directly underneath your navel to help you focus.

Pay conscious attention to your five senses. Take a moment to notice what you feel, hear, see, taste, and smell. Don't judge or label anything. Just notice. Consciously take it in. Do this for a couple of seconds for each of your senses.

Finally, soften and relax your eyes and eyebrows. Softening your eyes brings you back to this moment and into your body.

Ground yourself

Being grounded means that you're mentally, physically, and emotionally stable. Literally and figuratively you stand strong. You can ground yourself energetically by imagining little roots shooting down from the soles of your feet, deep into the earth, like the roots of a big, ancient tree.

If that's too vague or you don't feel grounded yet, you can also jump up and down a couple of times. This brings your attention to your legs and feet, which automatically grounds you. Or consciously feel how your feet connect with the earth through your shoes or your bare feet on the floor.

Come from your heart

When you're grounded, centered, and present, you're also connected with your heart, and this helps to bring you in touch with your feelings, inner wisdom, and other people. To enhance this connection, bring your attention to the center of your heart and imagine how any tension in that area softens or opens up. Or think of something or someone you love very much, and feel this love deeply, especially in the area around your heart.

Connecting FIRST with yourself is a crucial practice. It's especially important to consciously connect with yourself before you interact with others. Why? Because:

- You won't lose energy in the interaction.
- You're open to notice what goes on in your body and how you feel during your interaction. When it's a loving connection, you feel more love. When something happens that crosses your boundaries or makes you angry, you're aware of it the

moment it happens instead of afterwards. It's easier to know how to respond. (Plus, you actually can respond now, instead of reacting or lashing out.)

- You won't unwillingly pick up the energies or emotions of others.
- You feel more alive!
- You feel a deeper connection with others and can have a more meaningful conversation with them.
- If you work with people, connecting with yourself first is an absolute MUST. In addition to the benefits I describe above, you're ALSO more effective at your work. You become a much better coach, healer, or mentor because you pick up more information. You can sense what goes on with others and get more (and more accurate) intuitive hits on what you should ask or do to support your client.
- You remain connected with your own wants, needs, and desires, and you can take better care of yourself.
- You're completely open to your intuition, creativity, inner wisdom, the needs of your body, and your power and strength.

Practice establishing a connection with yourself at the beginning of each day, and make sure it's before you talk or interact with anyone.

I do this almost every morning. When I forget or don't take the time for it, I always regret it. When I consciously connect with myself I experience flow and feel good. When I forget, I lose energy and often feel restless and unfocused. Try it yourself and see if you notice a difference, too!

Reflection

What would be different today if you connected to yourself first?

Divinely Selfish Declarations

*   I always connect to myself first, so I never lose myself in my interactions with others.
*   The better I am connected to myself, the deeper I can connect with others.
*   Being present and coming from my heart makes me a better person and a better coach (healer / mentor / trainer / etc.)
*   The more I am present and connected to myself, the easier it is to hear my intuition and to know what's best for me.

Chapter 6

Own Your Power

In subtle and overt ways, powerful women have been (and still are!) judged, criticized, and shut down. They're deemed less attractive and unlikeable.

Women—and with that, their power—have been silenced, oppressed, and treated like second-rate people for centuries. They're still not treated as equals in many areas around the world. Even in the western world, women are still struggling to gain equal treatment and equal pay.

Women are generally not encouraged to be powerful or strong. A strong boy is seen as a natural leader, a strong girl is bossy. An outspoken man is assertive and clear, an outspoken woman is aggressive and a bitch. To this day women are raised and expected to be the ones who nurture, care, put others first, and aim to please.

This suppression and conditioning has left its mark on all women, to a certain degree. You may not realize how you have given away your power, though, so let's explore some ways this might be happening.

Example one: making yourself smaller

- You sit on the train. A man gets on and sits next to you. He automatically spreads out. You automatically slide into the corner to make space for him.

- You're telling a story at a party / are talking in a meeting or another setting where men and women are together, and you get interrupted every few minutes by one or more men. You don't say anything about it.
- You walk alone in the dark. There's a shortcut to your home, but it's through a park. What do you do? Walk through the park? Or not? And if you do, does it feel safe? Or are you constantly on edge, looking over your shoulder to make sure no one's following you?

Questions

Do you sometimes make yourself smaller or more invisible?
If so, when does this happen and why?

Example two: not asking for what you want

- Instead of focusing your attention on the ONLY thing YOU are responsible for (being clear on what you want and asking for it), you focus on the very thing you have zero responsibility for or any power over: the other person's response.
- You worry about what they'll think of you. If they'll be willing or able to give you what you want. How they will feel. If they will dislike you or think less of you because you ask for what you want. If it will ruin your relationship. And so on.
- You look at it from all angles, sides, and perspectives—except your own.
- You end up not asking for what you want, toning down your request, or apologizing profusely for the inconvenience of bothering them with your request.

Questions

Do you always ask for what you want?

If not, why?

Example three: apologizing when there's nothing to apologize for

- Apologizing for simply asking a question. Apologizing for starting to talk at the same time as another. Apologizing for bumping into someone when both of you weren't paying attention.

Questions

Do you sometimes apologize for something that doesn't require an apology?
If so, when? And why?

Example four: undercharging and over delivering

- You doubt if your service or product is worth what you're asking for, so you keep your price low and give more than you're willing to give. There's nothing wrong with giving more than people expect or paid for. But do you give from a feeling of fear that you're not good enough? Or do you give from a feeling of abundance and trust?
- How do you know if you give too much or for the wrong reasons? Do you feel unappreciated, unacknowledged, underpaid, undervalued, or feel you have to work too hard for the money you make? Then you give too much and / or charge too little. Do you quietly resent your clients because you feel like they took something from you? Same story.
- Do you feel GOOD about what you give, and do you enjoy adding more value to what you already shared? Don't change a thing. You're doing what's right for you.

Questions

Do you sometimes feel like you give too much? Or do you feel unappreciated or undervalued?
If so, why do you give more than feels right for you?

Example five: not speaking out or toning down your message

You probably already know if you do this. Unless . . . you censor yourself upfront without recognizing you're doing this. Signs you censor yourself may be:

- You find it hard to come up with ideas for articles and newsletters.
- You struggle with what to say or how to say it.
- When you read your own articles / sales pages / etc., they feel a bit . . . bland. They don't sound like you.

Questions

Do you censor yourself? How and where? And why do you do that?

Example six: using minimizing language

- You "just" emailed to check in. You "just" called to ask . . . You "just" want someone to know that . . . The word *just* diminishes your power and confidence. Leaving the word *just* out of these sentences makes each sentence stronger and shows your confidence.
- Another way you minimize your language shows up in how you express your opinions. Do you say, "I think that maybe . . ." or do you say, "I believe that . . ."?

Do you say, "I hope you don't mind me saying . . . ." or do you cut straight to the chase?

Do you say, "Not to offend or criticize you, but I have a slightly different view on this," or do you say, "I believe it's more like this."?

I know is more powerful than *I think*.

I'm convinced is more powerful than *I feel*.

I'm confident is more powerful than *I believe*.

You can't always replace one with the other, but pay attention to your language and see where your words could be stronger and think about why you minimize your message.

Questions

Do you sometimes use minimizing language?

Why? What are you trying to avoid or prevent?

Example seven: letting others take credit for your ideas or suggestions

If you've ever worked in an office or have been in some kind of meeting, you've probably seen this: a woman (you) brings up a point and it's ignored or dismissed. A man brings up *that same point* later, and now it's a great idea.

Most women have experienced or witnessed this. The thing is, what did you do when it happened? And what will you do if it happens again? Will you let others take credit for your input, let them talk over you, and ignore you or . . . will you demand to be listened to and given credit for your ideas?

Questions

Do you let others take the credit for your work?

Do you let others talk over you or ignore you?

Why? What are you avoiding or what are you afraid of?

Example eight: diminishing your results / not taking credit for your success

If you call it a coincidence, a fluke, or a stroke of luck, that's not taking credit for your success. Another way you can diminish your success is by saying it was no big deal or it was a team effort. Even if it was, YOU still did an outstanding job. Own it. You're not bragging or being arrogant. You're owning your value, power, and success.

Questions

Do you diminish your results or success?
Why?

Example nine: choosing to be liked over being effective or doing the right thing for yourself or your business

This happens when you don't fire someone because you're afraid they'll get mad at you; when you accept subpar work because you think it's not nice to ask for a higher standard; when you don't send back your nearly raw chicken because you don't want to hurt the chef's feelings.

Questions

Do you sometimes choose to be liked over speaking your truth or getting what you want or need?
Why?

Reflection

If you completely owned your power, what would be different?

Divinely Selfish Declarations

* I stop shrinking myself today.
* I'm comfortable with my power.
* It's safe for me to own my full power and express it, too.
* I'm excited to see how powerful I truly am!
* I'm a powerful being, and I'm in charge of how I use my power.
* I use my power for good, in alignment with my values and beliefs.
* I embrace all of my power.

Chapter 7

Honor Your Truth

To honor yourself and put your soul first, you first need to honor your truth.

We each have our own truth. What's true for me is not necessarily true for you. What's right for you may be wrong for me. What works for me may backfire for you. Even when something works for six billion others, that STILL doesn't mean it works for you, too.

Listen to your gut. Pay attention to your feelings and intuition. Notice how your body responds to what happens around you. These are signs and signals that tell you what's right for you and what isn't. This may take some conscious practice, though. We've unlearned how to be in touch with what we feel. We've unlearned how to express and honor our feelings. By not rocking the boat, by fitting in, and by pleasing others, we learned to override our feelings.

Dare to live your truth, even when it feels uncomfortable at first. But you can only honor what you want and need when you can recognize what they are. So start practicing. Notice how you feel, and practice acting on your truths.

When something makes you feel bad, or triggers resistance, or feels off to you, explore why that is. Usually, this happens for one of the following reasons.

- Something isn't good for you.

- This is not the right path or action for you.
- This won't work for you. OR
- A deeper fear or pain is being triggered and you need to look at that first.

You can uncover why something feels off for you by asking yourself these questions:

- What's happening?
- Why does this feel off to me?
- What's going on here?

When something makes you feel good, resonates deeply with you, triggers excitement or joy, and feels right? This is right for you. This is good for you. This is true for you. When something makes you feel lighter and better, it's true for you. When something makes you feel heavier and worse, it's not true for you.

It's important to *act* on what's right for you, too. Even when that makes you feel uncomfortable, scares you, or triggers doubts. Ignoring your truth NEVER works, as you've probably already experienced. So you may as well bite the bullet and honor what's right.

Don't blindly follow what others do, say, or believe. ALWAYS make sure something feels true for you. If it is so, go ahead. If not, do what feels right for YOU. It doesn't matter what others think about it. It only matters what *you* think about it.

Recognizing your truth can be difficult sometimes. One area where it took me a long time to realize my truth was marketing. I didn't like everything I learned about marketing, but I thought others knew better because their results were better. I tried working with joint venture partners for example. I didn't like it, but my coach at the time gained massive results with it. So I gave it a try anyway. Turned out, it didn't work for me. Not because I didn't do it right, but because this strategy was simply not a good fit for me. For my coach, it was true that this was a fantastic marketing tool. For me it's true that it wasn't.

Reflection

Where are you following what others do or say, even though it doesn't feel good to you?
What would feel better instead?
Take a deep breath . . . and do that.

Divinely Selfish Declarations

* I always know what's best for me.
* I trust myself and my inner compass above everything and everyone else.
* I always honor my truth, regardless of what others think about it.
* When I honor my truth, I honor my soul. When I honor my soul, I'm honoring my purpose. When I honor my purpose, I'm making the best of my life doing what I was born to do.
* Everyone has their own truth. I respect other people's truths and always act on what's true for *me*.

Chapter 8

Let Go of Shame

Shame is a debilitating and disempowering emotion. It can lead to self-destructive behavior. Whatever you're ashamed of, it doesn't serve you, and it's time to let go of it. Shame serves no purpose. Shame is often used by others to force you into obedience or to manipulate you. The results of being shamed can negatively impact you for a long time.

The good news is you can let go of shame and heal yourself so you're free to be true to yourself and put yourself first. The tips below can help. They certainly helped me to let go of feeling ashamed of needing so much alone time. How could it be that I love working with people, but feel fed up with people when I have too much interaction? I wondered if maybe there was something wrong with me or if I was doing something wrong. I wasn't. I only internalized criticism from others and started to feel shame as a result.

Forgive yourself (and perhaps others)

Forgive yourself for whatever it is you feel ashamed of. Forgive yourself for feeling ashamed.

Maybe you also need to forgive others. If so, three things are important. One, *only* forgive someone when you're *truly* ready to do so. If you still feel anger or resentment, it's too soon to forgive others. You need to tend to your feelings first.

Two, forgiveness is something you do for YOU, not something you do for another or to give them a get-out-of-jail-free card. You forgive someone because *you* no longer want to carry the burden of your anger, resentment, or pain. The other person doesn't even have to know you forgave them.

And three, you can forgive, but that doesn't mean you have to forget.

Be gentle with yourself

Have compassion with yourself. Treat yourself like you'd treat your very best friend. Change your self-talk. Don't shame or curse yourself. Stop judging yourself harshly. What would you say to someone you deeply love and respect? Tell yourself that.

Let go of what others think about you

Don't allow others to shame you. Know that they only do that because they need something from you, or because they're projecting their own, unhealed pain onto you.

None of that has anything to do with you, so there's no reason for you to accept the shame they try to place on you. Set boundaries if necessary and don't let them guilt-trip you into doing something you don't want to do.

Look at the positives

Focus on things you like about yourself. Shame is always triggered by negative self-talk. It can't survive in an atmosphere of love and appreciation.

Don't put others above you and don't put yourself above others

You are valuable and important. Other people may be smarter than you or better at performing some tasks, but that doesn't make them better people. There's never *any* reason to feel ashamed of who you are or feel like you are worse (or better!) than another. You may have been taught to believe that you're better or worse than another—but you're not. You are just as valuable, loveable, and worthy as everyone else.

Accept what has happened

You can't change what you did in the past. You can either forgive yourself or continue to beat yourself up. Is there something you can do today to make it better? Do it. Is there nothing you can do? Stop thinking about it. Why do you continue to punish yourself? Be kind and let go.

Reflection

Is there something you feel ashamed of?
What could help you let go of that?

Divinely Selfish Declarations

* I forgive myself for everything I did wrong or regret.
* I always learn from my mistakes.
* I treat myself with kindness, love, and respect.
* There is never any reason to be ashamed of who I am.

Chapter 9

Let Go of Guilt

Like shame, guilt is a debilitating feeling. Letting go of it brings you relief and frees up a lot of energy.

The tips that help you let go of shame also help you let go of guilt. There is, however, something else to pay attention to, and that is if your guilt is caused because of something you did wrong.

There's a difference between feeling guilty because you can't live up to another's expectation of you (that's not your responsibility and nothing to feel guilty about), and feeling guilty because you totaled your friend's car and didn't own up to it.

If you feel guilty because you did something wrong, you can't just shake it off. You need to make amends, too. Whether it's apologizing, telling the truth, or correcting a mistake: do that. It's the decent thing to do—and it might haunt you if you don't.

If you feel guilty about something, the first thing to do is to check why that is.

- Did you do something wrong? If so, can you still correct it?
- Could you have done something different?
- Would you *truly* have *wanted* to do something different?
- If there's nothing you could have done differently, forgive yourself, and let go.

Guilt, like shame, is often used as a tool to get you to obey or fall in line. As a result, you may carry around guilt that has NOTHING to do with what you did or didn't do, but is purely a projection of another's expectation, emotion or agenda. This isn't about you. You did nothing wrong, and there's nothing wrong with you. Be compassionate and kind to yourself. And be kind to others, too: don't use shaming, blaming, or other emotional manipulation to get your way or discipline others, either!!

Reflection

If you let go of your guilt, what would be different?

Divinely Selfish Declarations

* Making a mistake does not make me a bad person.
* I can do something wrong, but that doesn't mean there's something wrong with who I *am*.
* I treat myself and others with kindness and respect.
* I never have to feel guilty for being true to myself.
* There's no reason to feel guilty when others don't approve of who I am or what I do. That's their problem, not mine.

Chapter 10

Stop Toning Down Your Personality and Stop Being Someone You're *Not*

You don't have to change who you are to please others or to avoid ruffling someone's feathers. You don't have to mute your personality or character traits for fear that you're too much. Be YOU. In all of your glory and flaws.

Can there be situations where you (temporarily) adjust a little? Of course. You may want to stop cracking jokes when someone's delivering an emotional speech. You may want to let someone finish their story before you blurt out your own. But that's just common courtesy. That's not what I'm talking about. I'm talking about changing yourself into someone you're not.

If others can't cope with who you are, don't change who you are. Change your environment instead. Ignore people who expect you to be different. Surround yourself with people who love you *because* of who you are, not in spite of it. There are almost eight billion people on this planet. I'm pretty sure you can find a handful of them who love you for who you are.

The more you are true to yourself, without muting yourself or your opinions, the more your *true* friends will love you. The more your ideal clients will adore you. The easier it is to attract like-minded people, clients, and (business) opportunities that help you grow your business.

Growing your business and growing into the next-best version of yourself *always* requires you to be even MORE true to yourself. To be even more YOU. To let go of more things that aren't aligned with you. To let go of more of whatever you are NOT, and to embrace even more of who you truly are and dream of being. To let go of more shrinking or hiding behaviors. I notice it every time I go for a new goal or next level in my business: this ALWAYS involves being even more true to myself, my soul, my desires, and my dreams.

The world doesn't need you to be someone you're not. Everyone else is already *not* you. The world needs you to be YOU. YOU need you to be YOU.

Reflection

If you muted nothing about yourself and if you trusted it was safe to do so, what would you do or say today?

Divinely Selfish Declarations

* All I have to do is to be MORE of me, not LESS of me.
* The more ME I am, the easier it is to grow my business and attract my ideal clients.
* The more ME I am, the more the right people will like and love me.
* All I have to do is to be all that I am.

Chapter 11

Self-Love

Before we look at how you can learn to love yourself more (starting with *liking* yourself more, if loving yourself feels like a step too far), let's first look at why it's important to love yourself.

Self-destructive habits fall away when you love yourself. Because when you *truly* love yourself, how can you judge yourself critically and tell yourself you're not good enough? Self-loathing and self-hate fall away—and with them all the behaviors that are unhealthy, unloving, and bad for you. Your self-talk improves. Your inner critic no longer tortures you with endless talk on how bad, stupid, or unworthy you are. You see yourself as worthy to receive love, happiness, and everything else you desire. So you'll no longer sabotage receiving what you want.

You're more confident when you love yourself, and more powerful. Other people's opinions of you don't matter that much anymore. You accept yourself and have more faith in yourself. Your whole life lights up when you treat yourself with more love and compassion. Your emotional, spiritual, mental, and physical health improve. You look at the world from a different, more loving perspective. This not only makes the world seem like a better place, you're actively contributing to making it a better place, too! Because you love yourself more, the energy you radiate is filled with more love. Because you have more compassion for yourself, you can have more compassion for others. Because you love yourself more, your capacity to love others is enhanced as well. You treat yourself with more kindness and respect, and you automatically treat others with more kindness and respect, too.

So how do you DO it? How do you like, and even love, yourself more?

Before we dive into that, there's one more thing you need to know first: what self-love really means. It means to accept yourself with all your flaws and shadows. You know what you're good at and you also know where you need to learn more. Self-love means you fully accept and embrace EVERY part of yourself. You don't punish yourself or think there's something wrong with you. That's what I mean by self-love. That's what I invite you to learn and cultivate. I'm NOT asking you to become a pompous, arrogant, narcissistic ass. On the contrary! I'm inviting you to become a better, more loving person to yourself, and with that, to others, too.

Now we've got that out of the way, let's look at how you can practice liking and, ultimately, loving yourself more.

Accept and embrace every part of yourself

Self-acceptance is self-love in action. So is letting go of guilt, letting go of shame, and forgiving yourself. I had to learn to accept my introverted side. I believed there was something wrong with that for a long time. I no longer feel guilty or ashamed about that part of me. On the contrary! Now I even see it as a gift and my superpower. :-)

Excellent self-care

Take excellent care of yourself and prioritize your well-being. This works both ways. Once you love yourself more, you automatically take better care of yourself. Taking better care of yourself automatically leads to loving yourself more.

Stand up for yourself

Speak up. Be assertive. Ask for what you want and need. Don't let others walk over you. Don't accept being treated like shit. Set boundaries. Say NO to things you don't want or don't like.

Spend time with people you love

Stop hanging out with people who don't love you. Or seriously reduce the amount of time you spend with them.

Honor your feelings and truths

Listen to them. Act accordingly.

Live in alignment with your values

When you don't live according to your own values, you go against what deeply matters to you. That's a painful way to live and a betrayal of what's important to you.

Live the way you want to live

Don't change who you are or what is important to you in order to avoid confrontation with others. Don't live to please others or live the way they want you to live. Live to be you and live YOUR own life.

Say yes to your dreams

Say yes to your soul. Say yes to your desires. Say yes to what you want and need.

Say no to what you no longer want or accept

Give yourself what you need and stop tolerating what's not good for you.

Treat yourself like you'd treat someone you deeply love

How do you treat your best friend? What would you tell her if she came to you with the problem you have? How would you respond to a story she shares or an experience she's been through? Treat yourself like that.

The most important way to love yourself more is to put self-love in action. The moment you notice that you're unkind to yourself, stop and ask, What would love do now? If I truly loved myself, what would I do next? And do that.

Reflection

If you loved yourself deeply, what would change in your business and life?

> *Divinely Selfish Declarations*
>
> * I like who I am.
> * I treat myself like I treat my best friend: with kindness, love, and respect.
> * I'm patient and compassionate with myself.
> * I allow myself to make mistakes and be imperfect.
> * I love and accept myself more and more each day.
> * The more I love myself, the more I love others.

Chapter 12

How to Cut People Out of Your Life

Sometimes it's necessary to cut people from your life. Sometimes the relationship has run its course, and in that case, you can usually let your connection fizzle out. Sometimes people are no longer good for you. They don't treat you right, they hold you back, or they are toxic for you. It's time to say goodbye. Here's how you can do that.

The inner aspect first

Explore your feelings, motives, stories, and thoughts.

- What is it you no longer like or accept about this person or relationship?
- How is this person hurting you?
- How does that make you feel?
- What does it cost you to keep this person in your life?
- What makes it difficult to cut them from your life? What are you afraid of? What are you telling yourself? What do you fear will happen when you break up with them?
- How will it feel if they're no longer in your life? What will you gain? How much better will you feel? What do you no longer have to do or put up with once they're out of your life?

Heal what needs healing. Forgive yourself. If needed, and only if you feel up to it, forgive the other person. Work through your emotions so you don't dump them on that person and your conversation ends in a shouting match or a shame-and-blame game. Untangling your thoughts and emotions beforehand helps you break up in a good way.

Then, the breakup

After you have explored your thoughts and feelings, it's time for the breakup. You can do it by phone, letter, email, or face-to-face. The best way will depend on what feels best AND honors the relationship you had. If your contact mainly took place over the phone, it's okay to break up over the phone. If you're living together, it makes sense to do it face-to-face.

What you tell them and how you tell it is completely up to you. Just be as respectful as you can. And remember that you do NOT have to:

- Defend your decision. You have the right to make whatever decision you want. You don't have to justify it.
- Make them understand you. That's impossible. You can do your best to be as clear as possible, but that doesn't mean they'll understand you. Don't strive to be understood. Strive to be clear, kind, and respectful. Or whatever else feels important to you.

Speak from your heart about yourself, your emotions, and your perspective instead of pointing the finger at the other person. Talk about your own feelings and don't tell them what to feel or how to respond.

I once broke off a friendship because I felt she wanted more from me than I wanted to give. Our friendship felt unbalanced. She constantly expected more support, more attention, and more time with me. That didn't feel good. She acted like her well-being depended on me, and it felt like she wanted me to save her. That's not my job and that's exactly what I told her. I didn't say, "You want too much from me and are too demanding." I expressed what I felt and how I experienced our friendship. And I told her I no longer wanted to maintain a friendship with her.

The best thing to do is to be clear and upfront—again, as respectfully as you can. Come from your heart. Be grateful for what was, the fun you had (if any), and what you shared.

When I look back at the people I cut from my life, I'm still grateful for what they once meant to me. There's just no longer a place for them in my life today. We've grown in different directions. That's part of life. Some people stay with you for a lifetime and others for a short while. It's all good. They had their role to play, and it's played out now. The moment that soul-contract is fulfilled, the relationship can dissolve to make space for new people who are the perfect match for who you are today and where you're going next.

Grieve if you need, celebrate, and honor what was, and allow yourself to move on. Some people no longer have a place in your life, and it's okay to let them go.

Reflection

Are there people you'd like to cut from your life? Why?
How would your life be better if you did?

Divinely Selfish Declarations

* I'm worthy of having people in my life who treat me with love and respect.
* It's okay to let people go.
* I love and honor myself enough to surround myself with people who support me and love me for who I am.
* I decide how I want to be treated and accept nothing less from anyone.
* People who aren't good for me have no place in my life.
* When a soul-contract is fulfilled, the relationship dissolves. That's what's best for both of us.

Chapter 13

Trust Yourself

When you trust yourself, that means you believe that you're able to handle whatever happens. You trust your decisions, actions, wisdom, and intuition. You trust you'll be okay no matter what. You trust what you do and how you do it.

When you trust yourself, there's no need to compare yourself to others. You don't need anyone's validation or approval. Why would you need that? You trust yourself, your path, who you are, and what you do. This serves you tremendously in your business and life. Plus, you need to have faith in yourself to be true to your soul and your path.

Trusting yourself is something you can learn, practice, and develop. It doesn't matter how much you already trust yourself, you can always deepen it. The exercises below help you with that.

Where do you already trust yourself?

- In what area(s) of your life do you have complete faith in yourself? Why is that? What do you think, believe, and do in this area?
- In what area(s) of your life do you lack faith in yourself? Why is that? And how could you apply what you do, think, and believe in areas where you already trust yourself to this area?

Make a list of at least fifty reasons you CAN trust yourself

- Look at your past. Look at every problem you solved and every hurdle you jumped. Look at everything you learned and accomplished. (And feel free to add new things to this list each day: how did you prove you can trust yourself today?)
- Next, look at HOW you did that. What did you do? What did you believe about yourself at that time? What were you thinking or feeling? What did you let go of? What helped you fix or solve the problem? How did you achieve the results you were looking for?
- Hold on to this list. Read through it the moment you start to question yourself. It's a powerful reminder that YES, you can trust yourself completely!

I used to distrust my own wisdom when it came to growing my business. I struggled to get my business off the ground, which made me doubt my abilities as an entrepreneur. As a result, I sometimes followed other people's advice instead of listening to my intuition. I figured they knew better because their results were better.

When following other people's teachings still didn't bring me the results I craved, I started listening to my own wisdom instead. This had always served me well in my personal life, so why would it steer me wrong in business? Turns out, it didn't. Everything worked out better once I chose to trust myself and always follow my intuition. (And it feels MUCH better, too!)

Reflection

If you fully trusted yourself and knew it was safe to always listen to your own wisdom and intuition, what would you do today?

Divinely Selfish Declarations

* I trust myself completely.
* I am my own rock.
* I have full faith in myself.
* I've always been able to solve all my problems, so I'm confident I'll continue to do so for the rest of my life.
* I have every reason to believe in myself!

Chapter 14

Worthiness

A lot of women feel unworthy to receive—not only in general but also in specific areas of life. Some feel unworthy of receiving love. Others feel unworthy of receiving money. Success. Friendship. A beautiful home. Or happiness.

Not feeling worthy puts a limit on how much you can receive. It makes you settle, compromise, and tolerate things you'd rather not put up with. And it stops you from putting yourself first. How can you put yourself first if you don't think you're worthy enough to be prioritized?

It's not surprising many women struggle with worthiness. Women have been treated as second-rate humans for so long. There are many countries where women are STILL openly thought of as second-rate citizens. And even in western society, despite all the progress we've made, women still aren't seen, treated, or rewarded as equals. This has sent a message to *all* women that they're not as valuable as men. It's no wonder this can make you doubt your worthiness!

Every human being is valuable. *Every* human being is worthy to receive love, food, shelter, clean air, happiness, and whatever else you could want out of life. No one is worth more than another. Your value is a given. There's NOTHING you have to do to earn or prove that. We're *all* worthy, including you!

You don't need anyone's validation or permission to feel better about who you are. You can amp up your self-esteem all by yourself! Here's how.

First, *declare* that you ARE worthy and you don't have to earn the right to receive love, money, success, happiness, or anything else. Decide that you don't have to prove your worth to anyone (including yourself!). You don't have to *feel* worthy before you can decide that you *are*. You'll start to feel it *as a result* of that decision.

Next, start treating yourself in alignment with that decision. You can do that in the following ways.

- Treat yourself like you'd treat the love of your life.
- Give yourself as much care, love, and respect as you would your best friend.
- Stop criticizing yourself.
- Accept the fact that everyone is different and *embrace* what makes YOU different.
- Honor your successes. Acknowledge them. Don't temper any feelings of pride. It's okay to feel stoked about your results!
- Focus on what you like about yourself.
- Focus on what you did right and highlight that daily by writing down three things you did well each day.
- Every day write in your journal that you're worthy. Write it out in many forms.

Here are some example sentences to help you get started.

- I'm worthy to receive love.
- I'm worthy of success.
- I'm worthy of seeing all my dreams come true.
- I'm worthy of . . . (fill in whatever you desire.)

Write these statements down or read them out loud. The most important thing is that you let them sink in. Notice how it *feels*.

Reflection

What would change in your business and life if you didn't question your worthiness?

> ### *Divinely Selfish Reminders*
>
> * I am enough.
> * I am good enough.
> * I'm worthy to receive everything I desire—and then some!
> * I am worthy.
> * I AM.

Chapter 15

You Don't Have to Change so Other People Can Be Happy (and Vice Versa)

If other people aren't happy with who you are, that's too bad—but it's not your fault nor your responsibility.

You can't make others happy. Maybe you can temporarily, by doing something nice for them. You can say or do something that makes others feel good. But that's all.

If others aren't happy with who you are, that's their problem. If they demand you change because that would make them feel better, you don't need that person in your life. They don't really love you. Their "love" is VERY conditional. They don't love you for who you are, but for what you can do for them.

If others want you to change to make them happy, that's a) impossible, and b) super selfish of *them*. NOT Divinely Selfish. Not the soul, love-based kind of selfishness. No, it's the shallow, fear-based kind. Assuming you're not a sadistic serial killer (in that case, I understand why people would want you to change), you don't have to change who you are for ANYONE, EVER. You're meant to be exactly who you were born to be. If others can't handle that, that's their problem. Some aspects of your personality or your way of living can provoke something in them—something that needs *their* healing and care.

Even if you DO change to accommodate them, it still won't make a difference to their level of happiness, because whatever wound or thought made them feel bad IS STILL ALIVE INSIDE THEM. Your adapted behavior *might* not push their buttons anymore, but other people and situations WILL. That's why changing who you are can NEVER make anyone happy. And being true to yourself can't make another person UNhappy, either. (Again, assuming you're not a sociopath or someone who deliberately hurts people or animals.)

It works the other way around, too! You don't need others to change who *they* are for *you* to be happy, either. If someone mistreats you, set boundaries or kick them out of your life. If someone's true nature rubs you the wrong way, either find a way to live with that OR stop hanging out with them. No one can change who they *truly* are. Yes, you can change your beliefs, habits, and behaviors, but *not* your true self.

Your happiness is your responsibility. Other people's happiness is theirs. You can be the most loving person on the planet, and the people around you can STILL be and feel miserable. If you don't know how to be happy with yourself and your life, no one else can make you happy. It's. Just. Not. Possible.

Be who you are and let others be who they are. That's all you have to do. The people who truly love you love you for who you are anyway. They don't need you to change. True love never asks people to change who they are.

Reflection

If you truly believed you don't have to change who you are, what would change in your business or life?

Divinely Selfish Declarations

*   My happiness is on me; other people's happiness is on them.
*   I don't have to change who I am to make others happy— and others don't have to change who they are to make me happy.
*   My happiness doesn't depend on others.
*   Other people's happiness doesn't depend on me.
*   Being true to myself makes me happy!
*   It's okay to be true to myself, even if others have a problem with that.
*   I don't have to change who I am for anyone, ever.

Chapter 16

Allow Yourself to Have What You Really Want

There are two major reasons you don't always get what you really want. The first reason is that you're not clear on what it is you REALLY want. The second reason is that *knowing* what you want is one thing, but *allowing yourself to have it* is yet another.

There's so much to say on this topic that I dedicated an entire book to it already,* but I need to address it in this book, too. Because it's impossible to put yourself and your soul first if you don't honor your genuine desires. When you deny giving yourself what you want and need, you neglect your soul and you neglect your well-being.

Knowing what you want can be hard. Knowing what you *really* want is even trickier. And *having* what you really want? That can be even trickier still.

It's easy to lose touch with your desires. As you grow up, you quickly learn that things don't always go as you'd like and you can't always have your way. You need to go to sleep when you're not tired, brush your teeth when you don't want to, go to school when you'd rather play, and learn math even when you hate it. Later in life you have jobs to do and bills to pay.

All of this can make you lose touch with what you want. And even when you *know* what you want, you don't always allow yourself to *have* it.

So explore. Get back in touch with your desires. Don't settle upfront. These questions help you uncover what you truly want and how you can give that to yourself.

- If you could have *everything* you wanted, if anything was possible, if nothing scared you, and you trusted everything will always work out for you perfectly, what would you want for your life? What would you want for your business? What would you want today?
- How would *having* what you want make you feel? And how could you experience that feeling now?
- What would it mean for you to have the business, the life, the relationship you truly desire? How would that make you feel? How amazing would that be?
- What would it take for you to give yourself permission to have what you want? And how could you act on that now?

I denied myself what I *really* wanted for a while. When I first realized it was my dream to build a global business, it scared the crap out of me! At the time I was focused on working with clients in The Netherlands only. How could I reach people all over the world? This dream felt too big, too scary, and impossible to realize. So I tried to forget about it. But that dream kept coming back. Ignoring it became harder and more painful. After two years, the pain outweighed the fear, and I decided to honor my true dream. This was one of the best decisions I ever made!

Ever since then, I religiously check if what I think I want is the thing I TRULY want, or if it's a watered-down version of what I want. And I always choose the true desire. I know too well that settling for something less never makes you feel completely happy and fulfilled.

Reflection

If you believed you could have what you *really* want, what would change?

> *Divinely Selfish Reminders*
>
> * It's okay to want what I want and to have it, too!
> * I allow myself to receive everything I want—and more!
> * I'm worthy to receive and have everything I desire.
> * It's okay to receive more than I need.

———

*Book One in The Art of Divine Selfishness Series: *Unmute Your Life - break free from fear & go for what you REALLY want.* Full of inspiration, exercises, and journal prompts, this book will ignite your dreams and help you fulfill them. You can read all about it here: www.unmuteyourlife.com

Chapter 17

Do It For YOURSELF

Whatever you do: do it for YOU. Don't do it for others. Don't do it to please them or to try to make them happy. (Which isn't even possible, remember?)

Why is it so important to do things for yourself instead of for others? Because you do it *without needing or expecting anything from them in return.* You do it because it makes YOU happy. You do it because it lights YOU up. You do it because you WANT to do it. You feel FREE to do it. It feels good and right for you to do it, and that's why you do it. If your actions please others as well? Cool! That's a great bonus! But you don't *need* it.

Doing things for yourself liberates you: you do something because it makes you happy. You're not waiting to get something in return. You already got something in return: your happiness!

When you do things for yourself, this liberates other people. They don't feel any unspoken pressure or neediness from you. People ALWAYS feel when there are (emotional) strings attached to your action or gift. And it doesn't feel good. When you do something because you expect something in return and don't get it, you feel bad. You feel unappreciated and unseen. You resent the time and energy you spent, and you can even resent the person you did something for.

So stop doing that. Whatever you do, find a reason to do it for YOU.

Newsflash: you already do everything for yourself anyway, even when you think you do it for others! If you do something for someone hoping they'll like you, acknowledge you, or be grateful, you're not doing it for them. You do it for *you* because you think you need their approval. If you do something for someone, hoping they'll someday return the favor, you're doing it to get something in return. You did it for *you*. You only *told* yourself you did it for them.

When you do something to get something in return, no one wins. You're incorrectly thinking that you need to give something to get something. When you get it, you won't feel that you got enough or as much as you had hoped for. When you don't get it at all, you feel resentment and disappointment. The other person loses because they feel your unspoken neediness. They *know* you expect something back, but what? It's not clear. So they can't give it to you. That doesn't feel good.

Does this mean you should never do something for another person? Of course not!! Help others when you can, for sure! Just don't do it to get something back, unless you make a straightforward deal with the other person. ("I'll do this for you, but then I want this in return. Deal?")

Don't cross your boundaries. Don't give something you don't want to give. Don't burn yourself out being there for others. Don't do anything that makes you feel bad or feels like too much. Don't do anything that goes against your values. ALWAYS pay attention to your *true* motivation or ulterior motive or agenda. This way, you'll prevent disappointment and resentment.

Those times when you decide to do something for someone else, you can STILL find a reason to do it for yourself. It feels good to help a friend, for example. It feels good to return a favor. Do *nothing* if you're feeling resentment or it's against your will. Either find a reason to do it that genuinely feels good or don't do it.

If you're familiar with the Law of Attraction, you know that like attracts like. This means that the energy you send out is what you'll attract more of. So if you do something because you fear others won't like you if you don't do it, you'll attract more fear. If you do something because you need something from someone, you'll attract more feelings of neediness. Only when you do something out of love or joy will you attract more love or joy in return.

I very consciously do everything for myself. I wrote this book because I love writing and I love this topic. If you love it too, that's wonderful! It makes me genuinely happy when my books inspires and helps you—and that is definitely my intention. But I don't *need* you to love my book in order to feel happy, fulfilled, and whole. I don't *need* you to love my book to feel that it's okay to write more books. My happiness does not depend on what you think about this book, or me! My happiness depends on me, and so I do what makes me happy.

Reflection

If you stopped doing things for others and did things for yourself instead, what would be different?

Divinely Selfish Declarations

* I do things because they make me happy, including things I do for others.
* If I want something in return for what I do, I ask for it. I'm open about my expectations to myself and to others.
* I don't expect others to give me the feeling that I belong or that I matter. That's an inside job. If I can't feel that I matter or belong, no one else can make me feel that way. Only *I* can make myself feel that way.
* I don't do anything that doesn't make me feel good. I either won't do it or I'll find a way to feel good about it.
* I do everything for myself, and everyone benefits as a result!

Chapter 18

Courage

Putting yourself first takes courage. It requires you to say *yes* to things that feel scary and to say *no* when it feels uncomfortable. It requires you to stand up for yourself when you'd rather hide. Fortunately, you're stronger than you think. So let's start with looking at how courageous you already are. To do that, you can make a list of things you dreaded in the past but did anyway. Include everything you can think of: your first day at school, learning to ride a bike, jumping into the water from a high diving board, your first job interview, starting your business . . . anything.

Once your list is done, read through it. Look at it. Let it sink in that YOU are the one who did all this. All these things once scared you . . . and you did them anyway! Really *feel* that in your body.

Once you finish, you can then move on to the next step. It's a bit of work, but trust me, it's worth it! It gives you great insights into the actions and mindset that will help you overcome your fears. Answering the following questions will uncover these insights. Write down whatever you can remember for each item on your list.

- On a scale of one (not at all) to ten (full-on panic attack), how scared were you before you did this? What did you fear might go wrong or could happen?
- What made you do it anyway?

- What did you think that helped you do it?
- What did you feel that helped you to accomplish it?
- What did you let go of?
- What did you NOT do?
- How did you do it? Did you prepare, practice, ask for support, or jump right in?

When you look at your answers, can you see a pattern? Is there something you did, thought, or felt that seemed to work especially well for you? How can you apply these lessons to doing scary things now and in the future?

Answering these questions teaches you so much about yourself! How daring you are and more importantly, what *your unique flavor or bravery looks like.* Some people thrive on jumping in the deep end and taking massive risks. Others fare better when they take it step-by-step. This exercise helps you uncover your own recipe to a life where fear no longer stops you.

What also helps is to go over these questions when something you want feels too daunting.

- What will it cost you if you let fear stop you? What will it cost if you *don't* do this? How will that make you feel later? What will you miss out on if you don't do this?
- What will you gain if you do it? What will you win? What becomes possible?
- How will it make you feel to have done this? How will you feel about yourself?

It still takes courage to put myself first sometimes. I've practiced a lot and I'm good at it, but that doesn't mean it's always easy! I always do it, though. I learned the hard way that ignoring my needs and desires only causes me pain and exhaustion. That never makes me happy and doesn't serve anyone. The best way to make sure you can serve others as best you can is by being as true to yourself as you can possibly be.

Reflection

If nothing scared you and you trusted you were safe and that everything will always work out for you, what would you do or say today?

> *Divinely Selfish Declarations*
>
> * I'm much stronger than I think!
> * It's safe for me to do things that scare me.
> * I'm always safe.
> * I'm powerful, capable, and brave.
> * I honor myself and my dreams, even when it scares me. I know I can handle it!
> * The more courageous I am, the more courageous I become.
> * I'm getting stronger and braver every day, and the world is opening up to me as a result!

Chapter 19

Stop Comparing Yourself to Others

Comparing yourself to others is rarely constructive. Yes, others can inspire you. That's helpful. But when comparing yourself with others makes you feel bad or if it causes you to feel insecure or doubtful, STOP looking at what others do. Bring your focus back to the ONLY person who knows your path: YOU.

What's true for others isn't necessarily true for you. What works for others doesn't necessarily work for you. What makes others happy is not the same as what makes *you* happy. And what your soul came here to do, be, and experience is most definitely NOT the same as what anyone else is here to do, be, or experience.

So keep your eye on your own path instead of that of others. Let your soul guide you via your intuition, dreams, desires, and nudges. Your soul knows *your* path. Focus on that. What others do is their business and has nothing to do with you. What you do is your business and has nothing to do with others.

When you catch yourself comparing yourself to others, bring your attention back to yourself by answering these questions.

- What is this person doing that inspires you?
- What does that tell you about yourself? What does that tell you about your desires and what you want to achieve?

- What do other people do that annoys you or makes you feel bad?
- What does that tell you about yourself, your desires, your self-image and what you'd like to achieve?

Remember that you ONLY see the outside of someone's life. You only see what they choose to show you. It may seem like someone is always successful or always happy, but you don't know their struggles or how hard they had to work for their results.

If you want to compare yourself to anyone, compare yourself to *yourself.* To where you were a year ago, a month ago, a decade ago, and how much you've grown since then. How much stronger and wiser you are, and how much you've achieved and accomplished.

Reflection

If you completely ignored what others do or say, if you only focused on your path and what feels good to you, what would be different?

Divinely Selfish Declarations

* I do my thing and let others do theirs.
* I give myself full permission to carve my own path and do everything in my own way, regardless of what others do.
* I focus on my path and what feels good to me, and I don't get distracted by what others do or how they do it.

Chapter 20

Don't Let Anyone Tell You What to Do

Not your partner. Not your parents. Not your business coach, your best friend, the rest of the world. Not even me! ;-)

NO ONE. Take the advice and feedback that feels true in your bones—even when it's painful or hard. And dismiss everything else.

The only one who knows your path and truth is YOU. Be as stubborn and strong-willed as you need to be to pursue your path and relentlessly live your truth.

Reflection

If you ignored everything that doesn't feel 100% right to you, what would you do today?
What would be different in general?

Divinely Selfish Declarations

* I take advice from others only when it resonates with me 100%.
* I always think for myself and make up my own mind.
* I allow myself to be as stubborn and strong-willed as I need to be to live my life exactly as I want.

Chapter 21

Be Willing to Disappoint, Offend, and Disrupt

Your actions can sometimes disappoint others. Your actions could offend them. Or they could disrupt someone's plans. Even if you walk on eggshells and do your best to prevent disappointing people, it might STILL happen! People can feel offended by the weirdest things. That's not your fault. That's on them: a pain *in them* gets activated. Or they disagree with something you say and take that as a personal attack.

Treat others like you want to be treated. But other than that, be true to yourself and your truth, and don't be afraid to express it and live by it. Even when others don't like it.

Many years ago, I was still in the spiritual closet. I didn't openly talk about intuition or soul for fear of what people would think. I also I tiptoed around the term Divine Selfishness. Not the Divine part—I was cool with that, but the selfish part. If there's ONE thing that most women want to avoid like the plague, it's being called selfish. Even though I LOVED the phrase myself, I hesitated putting it in the banner of my website. I was afraid it would offend women and alienate potential clients. I was afraid it would hurt my business.

I got over that and now I use The Art of Divine Selfishness on my website and in my books. And yes, sometimes it ruffles someone's feathers. Several women have emailed me over the years urging me to rethink using the word *selfishness*, "Because that can be really off-putting." I never respond to those emails. Why would I? If they don't resonate with my message, they're free to ignore it.

Women especially have been raised to please others and been taught not to rock the boat. Expressing your truth and your opinion don't always go hand-in-hand with the status quo. As a result, you don't always say what you mean. You water down your truth or don't speak it at all. You don't share your opinions or you hide certain aspects of yourself. All to keep the peace and avoid conflicts. But in doing that, you betray yourself. Toning down some of you results in toning down ALL of you. You slowly lose yourself in that process.

I *get* it. That's why I shared that I'd been in the spiritual closet for some time and hesitated to use the word selfishness. I also wrote many blog posts that made me doubt if I *really* was ready to publish it. I STILL have moments where I write something and change it later, because I worry it was too bold or too in-your-face. I can express myself in not-so-subtle ways, to put it mildly, and I still take that out of my writing sometimes.

There's a fine line between expressing your truth in a way that's honest and pure and expressing your truth in a way that's unnecessarily harsh. I don't always know where that line is. Sometimes I'm too rash and sometimes I censor myself, if only a little. It's an ongoing process of being aware of my truth and being aware of when I am shying away from expressing it. And then . . . I express it after all. Because being true to myself and my soul is more important to me than not offending others, or potentially disappointing others, or hurting others' feelings. I'm willing to offend, disappoint, and disrupt to live in alignment with my soul, myself, my values, and my truth. Are you?

Reflection

If you were willing to disappoint, offend, and disrupt, what would change?
What would you say or do that you don't say or do now?

Divinely Selfish Declarations

* I give myself full permission to express myself and my opinions, even when others don't like it.
* I give myself full permission to disappoint others.
* I give myself full permission to rock the boat.
* I give myself full permission to offend others.
* I'm willing to offend, disappoint, and disrupt to be true to myself, my values, and my soul.
* It's safe for me to disappoint and offend others.
* It's safe for me to be true to myself and express my opinions and beliefs.
* It's safe for me to be ME.

Chapter 22

Follow Your Own Rhythm and Pace

Everyone has their own rhythm and pace. It's important to honor that if you want to put your soul and well-being first.

Some people are most creative in the morning, for example, and others in the evening. Everyone also has their own pace in learning, implementing, responding, acting, and integrating change. I'm someone who is always behind in online programs or classes, for example. I see others in the group move through the lessons and implement what they learn as they go. I'm never one of them. I like to take my time, and I don't act until it feels 100% right for me. Sometimes that happens quickly, and sometimes it never happens. But it's VERY rare for me to move along with the pace of the program.

This used to make me feel rushed. I felt I had to move faster, do more, and keep up! Not anymore. I've learned to honor my flow, regardless of what others are doing (or not doing). It doesn't matter what others do, how they do it, when they do it, or why they do it. I only listen to what makes sense and feels good to ME.

I'm never behind. I'm always on track on my own path. And I do what feels right in the moment it feels right. When I do that, I'm automatically honoring my own cycles of productivity and rest.

If you try to follow a pace that isn't yours or act before you're ready, it won't bring you the results you desire. It doesn't feel good either. You can only keep up by constantly pushing and pressuring yourself.

That's not productive, it wears you out, and it kills your creativity. What works best is to be true to your pace, your flow, your cycles, and your rhythm.

What you need to honor your pace is to listen to your intuition. It always tells you what to do and when to do it. Notice what you feel like doing and honor that as much as you can. And completely ignore what others do or expect from you—unless it aligns with what's best for you anyway.

These questions help you get clear on your rhythm and pace.

- Where are you pushing yourself?
- Why is that?
- Explore. Reflect. Is there something you're resisting? Something you fear? Something you think you may lose when you don't force yourself to do this?
- Where are you holding back? Why is that? What would you do if you didn't hold back?
- What does your natural rhythm look like? When are you most creative? When do you most feel like working out, doing creative work, being alone, or interacting with others? Are you a night owl or a morning person, or neither?
- Write down everything that comes up. If you're not sure about your answers, pay attention to all these questions from now on to find out.

Once you know what works best for you, you can honor it. Just remember to focus on yourself and what feels right for you. What works for others says NOTHING about what works for you, so there's no point in comparing your path to that of others. Give yourself permission to follow your own flow and to ignore everything else.

Reflection

If you were completely true to your rhythm and pace, what would you do today?

Divinely Selfish Declarations

* My intuition and what feels right dictate what I do, when I do it, and how I do it. What others do is irrelevant.
* I give myself permission to follow my own pace, regardless of how slow or fast that seems to be.
* I allow myself to follow my own flow.
* I build my business and life around my rhythm and flow as much as I can.
* I honor who I am, and how and when I work best.
* I know when to work and when to take a break, and I honor that as much as I can.

Chapter 23

Stop People Pleasing

People pleasing can take many forms, for example: not speaking up for yourself, saying *yes* when you want to say *no*, depleting yourself when giving to others, putting other's needs before your own, or doing something for another against your will. It's exhausting. People pleasing diminishes your power, shrinks your self-esteem, and makes it impossible to honor your wants and needs. Which also makes it impossible to honor your dreams—let alone to achieve them.

The truth is that you don't have to *earn* to be acknowledged, liked, or loved. You don't have to earn the right to be seen. You don't need other people's approval or permission to exist. People who love you only for what you do for them don't *really* love you. They just like what you do for them.

If you please others to avoid confrontations, it's time to learn to stand up for yourself and to stop caring so much about what others think. That takes practice but is a learnable skill. This book helps you with that. Learning to like, accept, and love yourself more will make a tremendous difference, too.

There are other things that help as well. We'll go over them in a moment. But first let's explore when and why you please others *at your own expense* to begin with.

- What, if anything, do you want in return for pleasing others?

- What, if anything, do you hope to avoid by pleasing others?
- If you're completely honest with yourself, what's the *real* reason you're pleasing others at your own expense? What is it you fear or resist?

If you don't know why you please others, ask yourself what you thought you had to do to receive love, approval, or recognition from your mother and / or your father (or whoever took care of you as a kid). Whatever it was that you craved from one or both parents is often something that still drives your behavior toward other people today. Once you know what you need from others, you can start giving that to yourself. The following tips help, too.

Know that you always have a choice

When someone asks for your help, this doesn't mean you have to give it.

When someone invites you to a party, this doesn't mean you have to go.

You're allowed to say *no*.

Take time to consider

When someone asks you something and you're not sure what you want, don't feel obligated to give an answer straight away. Say you need time to consider their request. How? Easy, just say, "I don't know yet. Let me think about it, and I'll get back to you later."

Allow yourself to disappoint others

There's an entire chapter dedicated to this topic, but I want to remind you of it here. It's truly okay to disappoint others!

You don't have to justify or explain anything

A simple *no* is enough. More on that in the chapter on saying no.

Pay attention to your real motivation for doing something for other people. Do you genuinely want to do this? Does it make you happy to help? Do you feel good about it? Go ahead. But when it depletes you, you don't want to do it, or you only do it because you're afraid of what might happen if you don't do it, then don't do it. When you keep giving what you don't want to give, eventually you'll resent yourself and / or others for it. You deplete and disempower yourself. And it's okay to stop doing that.

Reflection

If you gave yourself full permission to stop pleasing others, what would change in your business and life?

Divinely Selfish Declarations

* I give myself permission to stop pleasing others at my own expense. I don't have to do anything I don't want to do.
* I don't need others to see or acknowledge me, because I see and acknowledge myself.
* I respect and honor myself.
* I only please others when it makes me happy to do so.

Chapter 24

Know Your Non-Negotiables and Stick to Them

Sometimes it's okay to compromise. But sometimes it's not. Some things are so important that they're non-negotiable. You need to know what they are. That makes it easier to negotiate, to set and uphold boundaries, and to know when you can be flexible—or not. If you don't know what your non-negotiables are, you can unknowingly give up on them and feel bad, robbed, or resentful afterwards.

What I always find fascinating is how women are often clear on their non-negotiables for their *kids*, but for their own well-being and self-care? Not so much. They can be very clear, for example, that they don't allow their children over one hour of screen time per day. And you bet they stick to it! But when it comes to carving out time for themselves? That's rarely treated as a non-negotiable. If a client, kid, partner, friend, or family member needs them, their alone time quickly disappears. That's not sustainable long term. It wears you out and it just plain sucks if you are constantly giving up on things that are important to you.

Of course, you can only stick to your non-negotiables when you know what they are. So start there. These questions help.

- What's crucial for your self-care and overall well-being?

- What do you need to feel happy and fulfilled?
- What needs must be met for you to thrive? Make a list of everything that comes to mind.

Once you have that list, answer these questions for every item on it. Is this something you're willing to compromise on or make an exception for? Under what conditions are you willing to do that? Why?

After you've gone through your list, you know what you're not willing to give up on.

One of my non-negotiables is that I don't make appointments with clients before 10 a.m. on weekdays or at all on weekends. Another non-negotiable is that I *only* work with my ideal clients. Life is too short to spend it with people I don't love to hang out with. So I don't.

It may seem like these non-negotiables are about my well-being only. However, my clients benefit from them, too! Because I'm not at my best when I work at times or with people that aren't a perfect fit for me. *Could* I function when I have a client call on a weekend or work with someone I'm not 100% happy with? Of course I could. But would I be at my BEST? Only if I put a shitload of extra energy in my work and deplete myself. I'm not willing to do that.

Reflection

What are your non-negotiables?
What would change in your business and life if you stopped compromising on them?
How would you benefit?
How would others benefit?
How would your business benefit?

Divinely Selfish Declarations

* I know what I need and what matters to me, and I always give that to myself.
* I give myself full permission to never compromise on what truly matters to me.
* I owe it to myself to take good care of myself.
* I know what my non-negotiables are, and I stick to them, too!

Chapter 25

Allow Yourself to Be Angry

You're allowed to feel ALL of your feelings, including jealousy, annoyance, anger, and every other feeling you can think of. But what I've noticed in working with women, for almost twenty years now, is that they regularly feel ashamed of their feelings. They don't allow themselves to feel envious for example just because, "It's not nice to be jealous."

But there's *one* emotion that many women deny and suppress: anger. Because it's "just not done" for women to be angry. Women need to be polite, well behaved, caring, and kind. Women aren't supposed to be loud, assertive, and certainly not angry. Women are often seen as "too emotional," so most of us have learned to tone down our emotions or to rein them in. Especially in work environments or businesses, where you're expected to behave "professionally." So you can't be angry, because that makes you overly emotional, crazy, or a bitch. Or all of the above. Men can be angry and express it. No one will hold it against them, and in leaders, anger is seen as an excellent quality. For women, it's *still* not done. We aren't *expected* to express anger. Sure, within the privacy of your home, go ahead! But in public? Or in the workplace? No way. It's unattractive and not done, so you'd better not lose your temper!

It's unhealthy to suppress your feelings, including your anger. And there is ABSOLUTELY NOTHING WRONG with rage. Anger itself is neutral. Yes, it can be a force of destruction, but that's true for EVERY emotion. It's what you do with the anger that determines if it's *good* or *bad*. It can work wonders as an atomic force of creation and change, blasting the old to pieces and manifesting something new in a flash. Anger can be beautiful! It's definitely helped me to make major changes in my business, like making my business completely hermit-friendly. (Meaning I have all the alone time I want and need. I describe that entire journey in my book *The Happy Hermit*.) Being pissed off about NOT having enough alone time gave me an extra boost of energy through the process of making these changes.

If you don't allow yourself to feel or express your anger, it turns against you. It eats you up and festers inside you. So let's look at how you can make the most of your anger, because let's be honest: we're ALL angry sometimes. I don't trust ANYONE who claims he or she never gets angry. That person is a barrel of dynamite waiting to explode, and I'd rather not be near them when they do.

So how can you make the most of your fury?

Allow yourself to be angry

That, of course, is where it starts. Give yourself permission to be angry.

Get it out

Express your anger. You can shout and yell. (Not necessarily at others.) You can stomp on a pillow or hit a ball. You can also dance to loud music and shout along with it.

Write a letter

Write a letter to the person you're mad at. NOTE: you do NOT send this letter! Use it to express your rage completely uncensored. Don't hold back!! Cuss and be as unreasonable as you want. Just let it rip—but on a piece of paper you'll burn or shred to pieces afterward.

Vent to a friend

This is not the person you're mad at, but a dear friend who's willing to let you vent. Warn them upfront that it might get heated so they know what they're in for. The last thing you need is someone telling you to take it down a notch when you're in the middle of a good rant.

When you've let off enough steam to be able to communicate . . .

Talk to the person you're angry with. Tell them, in a healthy and constructive way, how you feel. Tell them what you're outraged about. Set boundaries if necessary. If their behavior has consequences, tell them what these consequences are. Stay away from blaming and name calling. However, if you accidentally blurt out what an asshole they are, well . . . it's not constructive, but it's not the end of the world either. Apologize and make up with them later.

But before you talk to them . . .

Be clear about what you want to get out of the conversation. Be honest about your expectations. Focus on what you CAN control (*your* behavior) and forget about trying to control what you have no control over (*their* behavior). You can set an intention to stay calm and grounded and clearly communicate your point. Remind yourself to keep breathing deeply while you speak. Promise yourself to be firm yet vulnerable. These are the things you have power over. However, wanting the other person to apologize, understand you, or kiss your feet and promise never to hurt you again is completely out of your control. So forget about that. This is why it's important to be clear about your expectations. Do you expect the other person to understand you? Well . . . that's not always possible. You can be crystal clear, but that doesn't mean others will understand you. Do you expect others will beg you for forgiveness? Well . . . you can be right and it might be justified to get an apology, but that doesn't mean you will get it.

When you have expectations about things you can't control, you make it harder to have a conversation.

It's better to focus on things you DO have control over. If, for example, it's your goal to express your anger and set a boundary, you set yourself up for success because achieving these goals are completely in your hands.

Be clear on what you expect of yourself. Speak your truth. Dare to be vulnerable and show others how they hurt you. Dare to be firm in drawing the line and setting boundaries. Dare to express yourself without hiding or dismissing your displeasure or other feelings.

Take a deep breath and have the conversation. It may be scary and hard, but it will empower you in ways that will positively surprise you!

Reflection

If you allowed yourself to be angry and to express it, too, what would be different in your business and life?

Divinely Selfish Declarations

* I allow myself to be angry and I give myself permission to express my anger in healthy and constructive ways.
* I embrace my anger. It's a powerful, constructive feeling that I use to change what I no longer tolerate. I use the energy of my fury to create more of what I DO want.
* I'm not afraid of my anger. It's a legitimate emotion, just like all other emotions. I allow myself to feel them all and am not afraid of them.
* There's nothing wrong with anger.
* I love my anger. It shows me what I don't accept and don't tolerate. It helps me take good care of myself.
* My anger is a force of good, and I use it constructively.

Chapter 26

Saying No and Accepting No, Too

Saying *no* to someone doesn't mean you are rejecting this person or their existence. It means you say *no* to what they ask of you. It works the other way around as well: when someone says *no* to you, they aren't rejecting *you* but what you asked for or suggested.

Saying no and *accepting no* are two sides of the same coin: both are important skills that are incredibly freeing. Being able to say and accept *no* can also bring you more opportunities!! When you're not afraid of *saying no* you gain more freedom. When you're not afraid to *accept* a *no*, your capacity to ask and receive more increases immensely. You'd be surprised at how much more you can get when you simply ASK more! These tips help you to say *no*.

Don't take or make it personal

You aren't rejecting the *person*, you're only saying *no* to their request. The same is true when someone tells you *no*. People aren't rejecting *you*. They say *no* because now is not the right time / it's not convenient / they aren't able to say yes. Whatever the reason is, it does NOT diminish your value or who you are. That's impossible! Don't make a *no* mean something other than it is. It's just an answer to a request. Nothing more and nothing less. The reason isn't even important. When others feel rejected, that's on them. When *you* feel rejected, that's on *you.* It's up to you to explore why you feel this way, understand which pain point gets pressed, and figure out what you can do to heal that.

Keep your answer short

You don't have to justify or explain your answer when you say *no.* Saying *no* is enough! You also don't have to apologize. If someone reacts angrily, is disappointed, or acts disgruntled, that does NOT mean you did something wrong or should have said *yes.* It only means they can't deal with your answer for reasons that have *everything* to do with them and *nothing* to do with you.

Three steps to say no

Step one—affirm the relationship and / or the question

Say something like, "How nice to hear from you!" or "Thank you for asking!" (You can skip this step if it doesn't feel right. Go straight to step two or three.)

Step two—thank them for the opportunity

Thank them only IF their question was indeed an opportunity! It makes sense to thank someone for asking if you'd be interested in speaking at their conference. It makes little sense to thank someone for the opportunity to carry their washing machine up five sets of stairs. Say something like, "Thank you for thinking of me," or "That sounds like a great opportunity." (Or skip this step and go straight to step three.)

Step three—decline

No wavering, justifying, apologizing, or explaining. Just decline. The short scripts below can help with that.

Short scripts to say no

- I don't have the time.
- I don't have the space.
- This is not something I choose to make time for now.
- No.
- I appreciate you asking me this, but I can't do it.
- I can't commit to that now.
- I understand you need help, but I'm not in a place to help you now.
- Can I get back to you on that? (This buys you time to feel your answer and muster enough courage to say no.)
- If you want an answer now, it's no. If anything changes, I'll let you know.
- I can't do this, but here's what I *can* do for you.
- I just can't right now.
- If the circumstances were different I'd love to, but right now, it's not possible.

Remember

You're already a PRO at saying *no*! How is that, you ask? When you say *yes* to a request to help someone out, you're saying *no* to time for yourself. When you say *yes* to watching a movie, you say *no* to reading a book. When you say *yes* to eating a bag of chips, you say *no* to eating an apple. When you say *yes* to going to a party, you say *no* to curling up on the couch with a glass of wine.

Every *yes* includes a *no*, and vice versa. They ALWAYS go hand-in-hand. The only questions are: what do you say YES to, what do you say NO to, and do your *yesses* and *nos* represent what TRULY matters to you, or are you giving in to others to avoid conflict?

Reflection

If you weren't afraid to *say* NO, what would you say *no* to now?
If you weren't afraid to *accept* a NO, what would you ask for now?

Divinely Selfish Declarations

* I'm a pro at saying *no*!
* I allow myself to say *no* whenever that feels right to me.
* When I say *no*, I am not rejecting someone, only their request.
* When someone says *no* to me, they aren't rejecting me, they're only saying *no* to my request.
* It's safe for me to say *no*.
* It's safe for me to hear a *no*.
* I allow myself to honor my needs and desires, even when that means I have to say *no* to others.

Chapter 27

Saying Yes

As we established in the previous chapter, it's not possible to say *yes* without also saying *no*, and vice versa.

It may seem easier to say *yes*—perhaps especially to specific people. But saying *yes* is actually a skill that needs as much (sometimes even more!) practice as saying *no*. Because most women have UNlearned to say *yes* to *themselves*. It's no problem to agree to other people's requests or demands, but saying *yes* to yourself . . . .?

It can be hard to say *yes* to your soul, your needs, your path and your dreams. It can be especially hard when you think saying *yes* might lead to conflicts, criticism, or negative comments from others.

Saying *yes* to yourself begins with giving yourself permission to do so. Being clear on what you *want* comes next. You always know—even if you think you don't know—what you want. You always feel what's right for you. The only reason you don't act on that is your fear of the consequences of honoring your desires This is how you can know what the best option is for you:

- Your *yesses* feel expansive. They bring you joy, open you up, make you tingle. You feel *good* and you feel like you have enough space.
- Your *nos* feel contractive. They close you off, you feel *off*, and they make you feel boxed in.

Allow yourself to feel what it is you TRULY want instead of living on autopilot. Allow yourself to say *no*. And allow yourself to say *YES*, too!! You always say *yes* and *no* at the same time anyway. Make sure your *yesses* and *nos* support the things that truly matter and make you feel fully alive.

Reflection

If you allowed yourself to say YES to your dreams, needs, wants, soul, yourself, and LIFE itself, what would you say *yes* to now?

> ### Divinely Selfish Declarations
>
> * I allow myself to say *yes* to whatever I want!
> * It's safe for me to say *yes* to life.
> * It's safe for me to say *yes* to MYSELF and to all my dreams, wants, needs, and desires.
> * My *yesses* don't need any justification or explanation. I never have to apologize for honoring myself, my needs, and my dreams!

Chapter 28

Your Core Values

If you want to honor what matters to you, you need to live in alignment with your core values. If you don't, something will always feel off. You'll feel bad about yourself, what you do, or how you do it. If you go against your values to fit in or make others happy, you'll resent them (and / or yourself) for it eventually. It's *impossible* to ignore your values and be true to yourself at the same time. Your values are a vital part of your personality, of your beliefs, of what you stand for. You must honor them in every area of your business and life. The key word is YOUR: it's important to live up to *your* values, the things that matter most to *you*. We all inherit and absorb values from people and society around us. But those values aren't necessarily the ones you care about.

There are no *wrong* or *right* values. There's only what *you* care about, and every aspect of your life should reflect that. If, for example, freedom is one of your core values, you won't thrive in a highly hierarchic environment. When one of your core values is honesty, your marketing needs to feel honest. When one of your core values is creativity, your work should feel creative to you. *Everything* should be aligned with your values:

- your friendships
- how you raise your kids
- your relationships

- your business model
- your marketing and sales process
- your website and its content
- your products and how you deliver your services or products

Assuming you're someone with integrity, including toward yourself, your values *matter* to you. It's important to check if you are living up to them fully, or if you could tighten things up.

This starts with knowing what your values *are.* So begin with writing down five to seven values that deeply matter to you. Think about what you care about when it comes to how you want to live, how you want to work, how you treat others, and who you want to be. What values does the best version of yourself live up to? Think about things like freedom, joy, love, creativity, spirituality, honesty, integrity, ease, flow, transparency, pleasure, connection, etc.

Once you know what your five to seven most important values are, go over every area in your business and life, and ask yourself if this area is aligned with each of them. Do you honor this value? How? Do you live up to it enough? If not, what needs to change? Answer these questions for every value and act on the outcome.

One of my most important values, for example, is freedom. So when I create a new online program I ask myself: does this feel free to me? From the price, to the content, to how I deliver it: does it feel completely free? If not, what needs to change? How can I feel even *more* free?

Answering these questions also changed how frequently I sent articles to my email list. I used to email one article per week on Wednesday mornings. For years, that routine felt great. Until one day I realized something felt off and I explored why that was. Did writing articles and sending emails still feel inspiring and creative? (Two of my other core values). It did. Did it still feel free? The answer was instantly clear: NO! I asked myself what would feel like ultimate freedom, and I knew right away: to send emails whenever I felt inspired, whether that was weekly, monthly, yearly, or sixty-five times per day. Relief!

I changed the frequency from once a week to weekly(ish), and now I enjoy sending articles again.

You don't have to go over *every* area of your life at once, of course. Just start with ONE area where something feels off. Ask yourself why it feels off. Check if each of your values is sufficiently honored. If not, how can you change that? What needs to change? How can you add more of each value to this area?

Reflection

If you honored your core values and lived up to them in everything you do, what would be different in your business and life?

Divinely Selfish Declarations

* I owe it to myself to honor my values.
* I always live up to what deeply matters to me, even when others don't understand or like it.
* My values are important to me and honoring them is an act of self-love.
* I honor my values in every area of my business and life.

Chapter 29

Don't Settle

People often settle for what they think they can get instead of going for what they TRULY want. Why do they do that? Because they're not sure they can have it, or are worth it. Maybe they're afraid to ask for too much, they don't want to seem selfish or greedy, or because something about their desire scares them.

Watering down your desires is rarely a conscious decision. It often happens in the blink of an eye, before a desire is fully formed. Your inner censor kicks in and before you know it, you've settled for something (or someone!) less than what you truly want.

Settling is not necessarily a bad thing, as long as you're making a conscious decision to do so. But when you give in, without checking that what you desire is *really* out of the question, you're selling yourself short. It's okay to ask for what you want, and it's okay to want more than you already have. It really is! You deserve good things, happiness, and good people in your life. Everyone does. You don't have to earn that right or suffer in one area to receive something beautiful in another.

Maybe you already know where you have settled. Maybe it's not yet clear. If not, pay attention over the next couple of days. Notice when you want to ask for something but don't. Notice when and where you lower your expectations or demands, and explore why that is.

Over the years I've seen my clients settle for numerous things like working with people who were not their ideal clients; working on days they'd rather take off; not having access to a quiet workspace, etc. They were able to change that *after* they decided to stop settling and gave themselves permission to receive something better.

You have full permission to ask for what you want. You may not get it, and the answer might be no. That's fine. But that's no reason to settle upfront. That's no reason not to even ask. You never know what's possible until you *ask* for it and until you stop accepting things you don't really want. Decide what you're unavailable for and what you ARE available for from now on.

Reflection

What would change in your business and life if you stopped settling?

Divinely Selfish Declarations

* I give myself full permission to ask for what I want.
* I don't know what I can get until I ask for it.
* I allow myself to get the best of everything.
* I'm allowed to express my desires and receive them, too.
* It's safe for me to *ask* for what I want.
* It's safe for me to *receive* what I want.
* I don't have to settle for anything (or anyone!) that doesn't make me truly happy.

Chapter 30

Prioritize Yourself

Prioritize yourself, your dreams, and your self-care. This does NOT mean you stop caring for others or become antisocial. Of course not! It's a common misconception that you can EITHER put yourself first OR you can be kind and caring. But you don't have to choose. You can do both.

Everyone understands that you can be there for others *more* when you take good care of yourself *first*. But in practice? Women tend to put others first: their children, parents, partner, clients, family, friends, neighbors, etc., and THEN—and ONLY then—do they feel free to do something just for themselves.

I know this is an exaggerated generalization. Or . . . is it? Do *you* put your dreams first? Does your self-care come before children or chores? Do you allow yourself downtime when your house is a mess, or if a client has asked for something? Can you relax when your to-do list still has items on it?

Of course there are situations, or even long periods of time, where you have to take care of others and there's not much time you can reserve for yourself. But you can *still* see where you can take some time for *you*. Five minutes of alone time is better than no time at all. Fifteen minutes of reading is better than no reading at all.

Prioritizing your dreams and self-care don't always take *extra* time. It's a matter of *choosing* what you spend your time on, and *how* you do the things you do. Are you busy for the sake of being busy, or do you take actions based on what TRULY matters? Do you waste time procrastinating? Do you lose time on social media? Do you spend hours on minor details that aren't important in the big scheme? Do you do things that aren't your responsibility, could be delegated, or don't have to be done at all?

Prioritizing your needs and your dreams begins with deciding that from now on, your self-care and what truly matters come first. You also need to be conscious of how you spend your time. Yes, sometimes others need something from you and this can't always wait. But often it can.

Give yourself permission to prioritize yourself. Decide that from now on your own needs, dreams, and desires are at the top of your list. Others benefit from that, too! But you're not doing it for them. You're doing it for YOU. And it's about time you gave yourself permission to stop letting everything and everyone come before you. It's your time now, baby. ;-)

Journal exercise

Make a list of twenty-five ways others benefit from you prioritizing your self-care, yourself, and your dreams. How do your children / friends / partner / clients / parents / etc. benefit?

Most importantly: how do YOU benefit when you put yourself first? Make a list of twenty-five ways how you, your health, well-being, happiness, zest for life, business, etc. will benefit.

Reflection

If you gave yourself FULL permission to prioritize yourself, what would you do today?

Divinely Selfish Declarations

*   I give myself full permission to put myself first.
*   My dreams and happiness are my priority now.
*   The more I am here for me, the more I can be there for others.

Chapter 31

Be Unapologetic

Women are conditioned to make themselves smaller, and more than just in the physical sense. They apologize for everything from the mess in their home to existing at all. They apologize for everything in between that, too. Apologizing diminishes your confidence and self-worth. When you apologize for something, what you say is that you're wrong: your opinion is wrong, what you did was wrong, or what you think is wrong. If you *were* wrong or you hurt someone, it's good to apologize. But it's unnecessary to apologize for anything else. That only keeps you small and makes you feel insecure.

You NEVER have to apologize for

- who you are,
- how you dress,
- what you like or dislike,
- what you believe in,
- what you dream of,
- who you love,
- the future you see for yourself, or
- what you expect from a partner.

You're allowed to take up space. To take a stand for your beliefs. To be who you are. There is NO NEED to apologize for ANY of that.

Notice when you feel like apologizing, and before you do, check if it's necessary. Is there *really* something to apologize for? Did you hurt someone? Did you make a mistake? Did your behavior negatively impact others? Was that your fault and responsibility? If so, apologize. If not, don't. It may feel uncomfortable at first, but you'll get used to it.

Also pay attention to your use of emoticons and emojis in your copy and emails, such as: ;-) and :-) When you overuse them, you downplay your message. Smileys can be fun, but they can also be a written form of apology. So notice where and *why* you use them. Do you use them to soften the blow, take off an edge, or downplay the importance of what you're communicating? Delete smileys when using them diminishes your message.

Reflection

Where are being you apologetic? Why?
What would change if you stopped doing that?

Divinely Selfish Declarations

* I no longer apologize for things I don't need to apologize for.
* I never have to apologize for who I am.
* I give myself full permission to be who I am without ever apologizing for it.

Chapter 32

It's Okay to Break a Promise

You make a promise with the best intention: to keep it. BUT . . . that's not always possible. Things change, you change, people change, situations change. You can't foresee everything. You can be absolutely certain that you can fulfill your promise but have to go back on your word later. That's okay. No one benefits when you begrudgingly try to keep your word. It negatively impacts you, your work, your mood, what you do, and how you do it.

I broke the promise to my editor when I worked on this book. After she sent me the first round of edits, I told her I'd send the manuscript back to her on January 11. But a week before that date I realized I wasn't able to make that deadline. So I broke my promise and asked to email the manuscript one week later. Thankfully, my editor could tweak her schedule and fit me. If that wouldn't have been possible, I'd still have sent the manuscript at that later date. I was willing to accept the consequences of breaking my promise because the quality of my book was more important to me than keeping my word.

Be careful about the promises you make. Don't make a promise if you doubt you can keep it. Mean every word the moment you speak it. Be certain about your motives and intentions: are you absolutely sure you want to and will, to the best of your knowledge, be able to keep this promise? If yes, then make it. If something changes and it's no longer possible to keep it after all? Give yourself permission to break it.

Yes, it's important to honor your commitments to others. AND it's equally important to honor your commitments to yourself. If this means you can't keep your word sometimes, so be it. Be open and honest and you'll be surprised at how well others take it. You may also be surprised how often the other person is looking for a way out, too!

Reflection

What, if anything, would change if you allowed yourself to break a promise or renegotiate a deal?

Divinely Selfish Declarations

* I give myself full permission to break a promise, to renegotiate a deal, and to change my mind.
* I honor my commitments and intentions, unless doing so is not in my best interest anymore.
* I only make promises that, in that moment, I am certain I can keep.
* I communicate clearly and openly about what others can expect from me.
* It's safe for me to change my mind or break a promise.

Chapter 33

You're the Boss

You're the boss. Of your business. Of your life. Of all your choices, decisions, and actions. No one else is the boss of you. YOU are.

Don't worry about being called *bossy*. That's a) not the same thing as being the boss, and b) a word that has been used to disempower women for centuries. Because it's "not nice" to be bossy. But men are *never* called bossy! When men act in ways that in women are described as *bossy*, it's suddenly described as "being assertive" or "being a powerful leader."

Screw whatever others think or say about you being in charge, because that's what you are!! You're the boss and in charge of yourself. If you're seen as bossy by some, so be it.

Your life is yours. It belongs to YOU and no one else. You're not required to check in with others, ask for permission, or discuss your life's decisions with ANYONE. Well, perhaps your partner if your decision affects them, too, but still . . . what you need to do to honor your soul and your truth trumps *any* claim *anyone* thinks they have on you.

The same goes for your business: it's yours. You're the boss and in charge. Not your clients, not your business coach, not your team, nope, YOU. It's time to fully own that you're the boss of YOU and *everything* having to do with you.

Reflection

What would you do today if you showed up as the boss and the person who's in charge?

Divinely Selfish Declarations

* I'm the boss.
* I give myself full permission to be the boss of my life.
* It's safe for me to own my power and be the boss.
* I'm in charge of myself, my business, and my life.
* I'm the leader of my life, not the victim of it.

Chapter 34

Screw the Rules

Some rules are good and it's wise to follow them. They serve you and others, they're ethical and moral, and the outcome of following these rules is good, too.

Other rules don't serve you. They serve others, they're unethical and immoral, or the outcome of following these rules is harmful. You don't have to follow those rules. It's up to YOU to decide which rules you follow—and which you ignore. I'm not asking you to start a revolution or break the law. I'm talking about spoken and unspoken rules that people follow without questioning them. They don't even question the point of the rules or if following those rules will actually be beneficial to them.

I'm inviting you to question *those* rules. To ask yourself if you believe in them, if they serve you, if this rule deeply resonates with you, and if you should follow it or not. These are rules about what to wear or how to act, what's done and not done, what's good and what's bad. These are rules about business, or writing, or doing *anything* that you're supposed to do because this is "just how it works" and "just how things are done." Is it?

When something feels off to you, question it. When you ask why something is done a certain way and the answer is "Because we've always done it this way," or "Because that's just how it's done," question it.

Never follow anyone or anything blindly. You have your own (moral) compass that shows you what's best for YOU. Sometimes what's best is to do the same thing others do. Sometimes it's not. The only one who knows what serves you best is YOU. Honor your own wisdom, intuition, and guidance—above the guidance of others. Honor your truth above that of others. Always think for yourself, never blindly follow the masses, and never go against your own instincts. When something feels off to you, something IS off. A rule may work for millions of others and still not work for you.

Question the rules and screw them if they don't work for you. Again, I'm not telling you to murder people or to stop paying your taxes. I'm inviting you to question anything that doesn't sit right with you, and to follow your own path always—even when that means you do things differently and don't follow the trodden path.

How do you know when it's time to question something? When something makes you feel less than good. When you have doubts if something is right for you. When you wonder if there might be a different way. When you think a rule is stupid or when something feels off.

I have no problem following rules as long as they make sense to me and they're aligned with my values. For that reason I have no problem with not killing anyone, for example. I don't need a rule for that, it's something I'd never do anyway. But when something feels even a little off, I question it. Two "rules" I consciously break are:

- That you can't curse or use the word "fuck" on a sales page or in your marketing. (I curse in real life, too, so once you work with me or purchase one of my programs, you'll hear me curse sooner or later. I believe that my ideal clients aren't that easily offended. Besides, they sometimes curse, too. So why would they care about my occasional cussing?)
- That you need professional pictures taken by a photographer for your website or the back cover of your book, or else people won't take you seriously. (Really? I think it's more important

that a picture shows your true nature and soul. The picture on the back cover of this book does. Nope, it's not taken by a professional photographer—Arjen, my partner, took it on a vacation in Greece. I like it and think it accurately represents who I am, so I believe it's more than good enough to put on my book and my website. I *may* have new pictures taken by a photographer one day like I've done in the past, IF I feel inspired to do so again at some point.)

I invite you to do the same thing: to think for yourself and to make up your own mind. Trust yourself when you feel something is good for you. Question everything that doesn't feel 100% right for you. And when something doesn't sit well with you? Ignore it and do your own thing.

Reflection

If you allowed yourself to do your own thing and screwed rules and customs that don't resonate with your truth, what would be different in your life? And in your business?

Divinely Selfish Declarations

* I always think for myself and make up my own mind.
* It's safe for me to screw the rules.
* I allow myself to walk my own path and do my own thing.
* Rules are meant to serve me, not the other way around.
* If a rule doesn't fit me, I joyfully ignore it.

Chapter 35

Fire Your Inner Critic

We all have an inner critic. It's the voice that tells you you're stupid, you look fat, you made a dumb remark, or you're not good enough. It's also the voice that tells you it's wrong to put yourself first and you shouldn't be so selfish. It's a cold voice without kindness or compassion. And that's precisely why you shouldn't take *anything* that voice says seriously.

It's good to be *critical* of yourself and what you do. Because you *can* make mistakes and there's always room for improvement and growth. But there's a difference between exploring what you might do better and burning yourself to the ground. There are gentle ways to see where you can improve or do things better. You can acknowledge a mistake without giving yourself hell for it.

Your inner critic *never* tells the truth. Its only job is to bring you down and make you feel bad about yourself. It has absolutely no constructive contribution to make. It's best to ignore her, to fire her, even! Or at least to fire yourself from the obligation of listening to her and taking her brutal comments seriously.

Replace the voice of your inner critic with the voice of your inner wise one. The one who can be critical but always does so with compassion and kindness. If you like, you can write your inner critic a letter of resignation. This can be a fun, symbolic gesture to let her know you mean business.

It can look something like this:

Dear inner critic,

You've been with me for many years now. In fact, you've made yourself heard for as long as I can remember. Your job has been to bring me down and ridicule who I am and what I do. And you did great! But as of now, your services are no longer needed. You're fired.

Thank you for your years of service. I wish you well.

Love,
Your name

Reflection

What would be different if you stopped taking your inner critic seriously?

Divinely Selfish Declarations

* I always treat myself with love and respect.
* My self-talk is loving, kind, and compassionate.
* I talk to myself the way I talk to someone I love with all my heart.

Chapter 36

Balance Giving and Receiving

The acts of giving and receiving are out of balance for many women. They give more than they receive. They give more to others than to themselves. They give things they don't want to give in order to get something they want without directly asking for it.

When the balance between giving and receiving is off, you eventually wear yourself out. You can start to feel resentful toward people who don't give you what you want, or feel short-changed in general. Giving too much is a massive energy drain. And if you give too much for too long, you can end up burned out.

Restoring that balance requires two things. First, you need to stop giving what you don't want to give. Second, you need to *ask* for what you want instead of assuming others can read your mind and will magically give you what you need. They *may* do that, but it's not their job to figure out what you want. It's *your* job to be clear about what you need and to ask for it.

When you find a balance between giving and receiving, you'll feel more energized. You'll be more fulfilled and happier in general. The more you receive, the more you can give. The more you give, the more you can receive—if you're open for it. You can give the best of yourself when you're willing to receive the best of everything in return.

It's important to give only what you TRULY want to give. Does it make you feel happy? Go ahead. Does it feel off or do you feel a hint of resistance? Stop and check what's going on. What's your *true* motivation? Do you want to receive something in return? Do you want to feel like a savior? Does your ego need the boost of feeling that others need you? Be honest. When your motivation to give is to receive something or to feel needed, something is off, and your motivation isn't pure. It's not rooted in love. It comes from scarcity and lack with a hint of emotional manipulation.

Explore why you give and if you allow yourself to receive enough. Do you charge enough for your work? Do you accept compliments fully or do you brush them off? Can you accept help? Can you ask for help? Can you accept favors? Do you feel good about receiving presents or does it feel uncomfortable?

Notice times when you'd like to ask for more but don't. Explore why you don't ask for what you want. Why is that? What do you fear? You're free to ask for whatever you want. You may or may not get it, but when you don't ask, you'll never know. As long as you're willing to accept a *yes* and a *no*, you're always free to ask. *You* can ask for what you want, *others* are free to answer what they want.

If someone asks something of you that you can't or won't give, be honest about that and decline. There's only so much you can give without wearing yourself out. By all means, give generously from the heart. As long as you receive generously, too.

Reflection

If you stopped giving what you're no longer willing to give, what would change?
If you allowed yourself to receive more, what would change?

Divinely Selfish Declarations

* I allow myself to ask and receive much more!
* I only give what I love to give.
* I ask for everything I want and need.
* It's safe for me to ask for help and support.
* The more I receive, the more I can give.

Chapter 37

Don't Be Afraid to Take Up Your Space

One thing I include in my private coaching is unlimited email coaching. I want my clients to feel they're completely taken care of during our time together and never have to wait for our next call before they can ask me anything. Nor do I want them to struggle alone when I can get them back on track in a couple of minutes.

What I ALWAYS have to do is encourage my clients to actually *use* the unlimited email coaching. What often happens is that my clients feel they can't take up that much of my time. They're afraid they're a burden or they bother me. They worry I might think they email too often. They fear that they're too much.

The overwhelming majority of women are afraid they ask for too much—even when they PAID me to coach them and the unlimited email coaching is included in their coaching package!

Chances are this is true for you, too. So take a moment to reflect.

- Do you sometimes think that your personality or energy may be overbearing to other people?
- Do you sometimes think that you ask for too much?
- How does this show up in your business / life?
- How does this negatively impact your business / life?

You're *not* too much. You're allowed to take up your space. Everyone is! You don't have to make yourself smaller for fear that you're a burden. How could your presence be a burden to others? How could you ever be too much? When others experience it that way, it's usually because something about you triggers a response in them. Maybe they'd like to take up more space but are afraid to do so. Maybe they want to be more expressive, but don't have the courage for it. Whatever it is, you're not the cause of what they feel. They felt that way already. Something about their interaction with you made them aware of it.

Reflection

What would be different in your business and life if you let go of the fear that you're too much or you ask for too much?

Divinely Selfish Declarations

* I allow myself to take up my space.
* I stop making myself smaller and allow myself to show up as I am.
* I give myself permission to be myself without restrictions, yet always with love and respect for myself and others.

Chapter 38

Take Full Responsibility

Taking full responsibility for your life means that you stop blaming others or circumstances for the conditions of your life. You take responsibility for your actions, thoughts, emotions, behavior, results, and happiness. You no longer act like a victim.

To be absolutely clear: you *can* be a victim!! When someone hurts or abuses you, you're a victim of their behavior. But there's a difference between being a victim and thinking or believing that others are responsible for the way things are going in your life. And it's the latter I'm talking about.

Taking full responsibility is not always easy. It requires a lot of emotional maturity. It's easy to blame others for how you feel. It can be hard to accept full responsibility for your life and yourself. But when you do . . . FREEDOM!

When I first learned that I was responsible for my own happiness and results (or lack thereof), I disliked that at first. When I felt wronged or hurt, it sometimes felt good to blame someone or something. But then I realized the power of taking full responsibility. When I'm the one who's responsible for my happiness and results, that means that I *never have to wait on others or circumstances to change to improve my life . . . it's ALL in my hands!*

Once you recognize that you're the one in charge of your life, you have access to your full power. When you take only partial responsibility, you have access to only part of your power. Gaining access to your full power is a form of self-mastery. It's incredibly empowering to take responsibility for your happiness, for your results, and for your life.

When you think others (or your circumstances) are responsible for your happiness (or lack thereof), you can ONLY be happy when others (or your circumstances) change. This makes you dependent. Your happiness is in others' hands and you're completely at their mercy.

But other people can't make you happy. Temporarily, yes, absolutely! They can do things that make you happy for an hour, a day, or maybe even a week. But NO ONE has the power to create a happy life for you but *you*. No one can bring meaning and fulfillment to your life but *you*. No one can heal you but *you*. No one can live your life for you but *you*.

Take ownership of your feelings, emotions, actions, and life. Explore what you think you need from others and see how you can give this to yourself. You can't receive from others what you can't give to yourself anyway . . . .

Reflection

Where are you blaming (or crediting) others or circumstances for your life, actions, results or how you feel? What would be different if you stopped doing that?

Divinely Selfish Declarations

* I take full responsibility for my life.
* I take full responsibility for the results of my actions and feelings.
* I take full responsibility for my business.
* By taking full responsibility for myself, I have access to my full power.
* I'm in charge of myself, my business, and my life.
* It feels liberating and powerful to take full responsibility for my life!

Chapter 39

Let Go of Responsibility

The previous chapter encouraged you to take full responsibility for yourself and your life. There's one more aspect to that, though, and that is to let go of *everything* you're NOT responsible for.

Just like *you* are responsible for *your* happiness, *other people* are responsible for *theirs*. You are NOT responsible for other people's happiness, well-being, health, wealth, etc. And just like you don't have to accept other people's hurtful behavior, you have no place treating others like crap. Not being responsible for other people's happiness doesn't give you permission to act like a jerk or take advantage of others.

You're NOT responsible for anyone else's well-being or feelings. You're not responsible for their results. You're only accountable for how you treat others. That's it. You have absolutely *zero* control over how your behavior affects others. You can have the best intentions and still unknowingly hurt someone. You can go about your day, minding your own business, and somehow hurt someone without realizing it.

It's not because of you that someone feels sad, mad, disappointed, inadequate, jealous, scared, or anything else. These feelings and pains were alive in them already. Your presence or something you said merely pushed the button that was already there.

Again, how you treat others, what you do, and how you do it is your responsibility. The consequences of your actions and behaviors are yours to deal with, too. But how others feel? What's possible for them? How happy they can be? How good they can feel? That is out of your hands and NOT your responsibility.

So let it go. Forget about everything you're not responsible for. You're not so powerful that you can make or break someone's life. That's not in your hands and be glad it isn't!

If you REALLY care about others and their well-being, LET them take responsibility for themselves! That's the best way to empower them. Besides, taking on the responsibility for someone else's life or happiness has NOTHING to do with your concern for them. It has EVERYTHING to do with fulfilling a need of your own. A need to be liked, loved, acknowledged, seen, or needed. It could be a need for others to follow your agenda. It might be a need for distraction from your own life. Or it's a need to control what happens, how it happens, and when it happens. These are just a few common reasons people take on responsibilities that aren't theirs. It may *seem* like a nice thing to do, but trying to control other people's responsibilities is disempowering. It shows a lack of trust. It says, "Let me handle this because I don't believe you're capable of doing this yourself." It is ultimately something you do for *yourself*, not them. Trying to control others is probably one of the most selfish things you can do . . . and no, not the Divine Selfishness that serves others and comes from love, but the shallow, ego-driven selfishness that's rooted in fear and lack.

Reflection

What would be different if you let go of making yourself responsible for other people's happiness?
How would it feel to let go of all responsibilities that aren't yours?

Divinely Selfish Declarations

* I'm not responsible for other people's happiness or well-being.
* The only responsibility I have toward others is to treat them as I want to be treated: with love and respect.
* The most loving and empowering thing I can do for others is to let them take responsibility for their own happiness and lives.
* The more responsibility I take for myself and my happiness, the less I feel the need to control others or meddle with their lives.

Chapter 40

Stop Caring about What Others Think

It's not always possible to stop caring about what others think. Sometimes it *does* impact you, especially if you've had a bad day, you slept lousy, or you're emotionally wobbly. Allow yourself to feel whatever feelings come up, but don't let others' thoughts or opinions determine your actions. Because it's not important what others think about you. It only matters what YOU think about you.

When you love and accept yourself, it doesn't matter if someone doesn't like you. When you feel good about what you have done, it doesn't matter if others don't like it. It's impossible to please everyone, so there's no point in trying. As long as *you* know you did your best, you're fine.

Besides, you have NO idea what others think of you, or if they think of you at all. You *think* they think something, but you don't know for sure.

Others are like you in that they spend 99% of the time thinking about themselves: their worries, issues, problems, and dreams. Most people don't care about what you do. They only care about how your actions affect them. But that has nothing to do with *you*. That has everything to do with *them*.

If someone says something nasty or mean, you can block or delete them on social media. In real life, you can ignore them or confront them. In both scenarios you can let them know you don't accept that behavior and delete them from your life. You don't have to accept crap behavior from anyone!

Ask yourself, Why does it matter what people think of you? Why would you let what others think of you influence what you do or who you are?

Go back to the chapters about self-love and self-acceptance if this concept is hard for you. There's probably more work needed in these areas. When you fully love and accept yourself, other people's opinions can sting or hurt, but they can't sway you from your path. What actually hurts you is when what others say about you resonates with your opinions of yourself. If you find it hard to let go of what you assume others think of you, it's time to explore what YOU think of you, and how your own thoughts are hurting and holding you back.

Fear of what others might think of me or my work was one of the main reasons it took me a while to write my first book. I was afraid no one would be interested in what I had to say (or worse, *dislike* it!). What helped me write that book was to remind myself of a vow I made many years ago: to live the life of my *dreams* instead of the life of my *fears*. It was my biggest dream to write books, so I finally chose to honor that dream instead of letting a fear dictate my life!

Reflection

What would be different if you never let anyone's opinion of you hold influence over you?

Divinely Selfish Declarations

*   I don't let what others may or may not think of me stop
    me from being who I am and doing what I choose.
*   What I think of myself is more important than what
    others think of me.
*   I always think good thoughts about myself.

Chapter 41

Stop Trying to Be Everything to Everyone

You can't be everything to everyone—and you don't have to be! Stop putting so much pressure on yourself to be the best friend, partner, daughter, sister, etc. Also don't be too demanding of yourself, and expect yourself to be loving AND caring AND kind AND compassionate AND strong AND courageous, and whatever else you feel you need to be.

It's not possible to be everything to everyone. It's not even possible to be everything to ONE person! Cut yourself some slack. All you have to do is to be YOU and treat others like you want to be treated. Period. That's all! When others don't love you for who you are, it's not really love.

People who don't love you for who you are will never love you, not even if you change, so there's no point to try to win their love. It won't happen and you'll burn yourself out in the process.

Surround yourself with people who love you as you are. Who treat you as you want to be treated. Avoid everyone else like the plague. You don't need them in your life! The beauty of having your own business is that you can choose who you surround yourself with. You get to choose who you hire, who you work with, and who you delegate to. It's ALL your choice!

You can't choose your family, so you just have to make the best of it if you didn't luck out in that department. (Although breaking off contact with your family is always an option, too—albeit not an easy decision to make.)

You also get to choose your partner and friends. So choose them wisely and carefully, too, and don't be afraid to be picky. Why wouldn't you? You're worthy of the best!

Reflection

If you allowed yourself to stop being everything to everyone, what would be different?

How would it feel if you allowed yourself to just be yourself around everyone all the time?

Divinely Selfish Declarations

* I allow myself to stop trying to be everything to everyone. All I have to do is to be me, always, and everywhere!
* I allow myself to be picky in who I allow into my life and who I spend time with.
* It's safe for me to be me, always and everywhere.
* I stop demanding so goddamn much of myself and cut myself some slack, starting now!

Chapter 42

Speak Up and Be More Assertive

Speaking up, sharing your opinion, taking a stand for what you believe in, letting others know when they crossed a boundary . . . these actions can trigger doubts and fears.

But you'll never feel free if you constantly swallow your words. In the short run, it can feel easier to shut up. In the long run, however, it's better to bite the bullet and speak out. So have that difficult conversation and broach that sensitive subject. It's okay to be vulnerable, to speak your mind, and to share what you feel.

Speaking your mind is NOT the same as creating conflict or being disrespectful or unkind. You can take a stand and be assertive in a respectful, loving way. You can be fierce and loving at the same time, too!

Notice when and where you hold something in and explore why you do it. This will show you what you need to learn to speak up. I used to shut down when I was around people who I thought were "above" me. People who I thought were wiser, smarter, or more of an expert. I figured I had nothing to add and was afraid to make a fool of myself, so I made myself smaller and didn't chime in.

I realized I needed to stop putting others above (or beneath!) me. Sure, someone can know more about something than I do, or be wiser and smarter, but that doesn't mean I can't have an opinion or offer something of value. And it certainly doesn't mean I'm less than (or better than!!) anyone else.

When you compare yourself to others and measure who's "above" and who's "below," this means only one thing: you need to work on your self-confidence, self-love, and self-esteem. When you feel good about who you are, you can accept others as they are, and you never feel better or worse than anyone.

You may have a different reason for not speaking out. Maybe the situation feels unsafe, for example—that's a common reason, too.

Explore what makes it hard for you to speak your mind and what you need to feel safe. How can you give that to yourself? What helps you speak out even when it feels uncomfortable or scary?

One thing that helps is to look at what it costs you to *not* speak your mind. It costs you peace of mind, frustration, feeling small and unfree, for example. Another thing that helps is to look at what it brings you when you do speak your mind. It brings you liberation, relief, more power, and inner freedom.

Start practicing speaking your mind more. Start small: share something you don't normally talk about with your best friend. If someone makes a joke you don't like, tell them. Share your opinion. When you notice you want to say something but hold back . . . take a deep breath and say it anyway.

When you start speaking your mind more, you will become more assertive and more powerful. There's always more assertiveness, more power, more honesty, and more vulnerability to sink into. You'll feel liberated every time you do. Plus, speaking your mind has a VERY nice bonus: you deepen not only the connection with yourself but also with others as well!

Reflection

If you weren't afraid to speak your mind and trusted it's safe to do so, what would you say and to whom?

> *Divinely Selfish Declarations*
>
> * I allow myself to speak up and speak out whenever I choose.
> * It's safe for me to speak my mind, share my opinions, be vulnerable, and be powerful.
> * I stop making myself smaller (or bigger!) than others. I am who I am, and I'm more than good enough.

Chapter 43

Boundaries

There's so much to say about this topic that I could fill a book with it. But I'll try to condense it into this one chapter.*

Let's start with why you need boundaries. You need them for the same reason you need to be Divinely Selfish: when you don't have boundaries (or don't stick to them), you can get angry or bitter. You might get taken advantage of. You'll wear yourself out and feel depleted. A lack of boundaries also leads to a lack of self-confidence and self-esteem.

Setting boundaries isn't always easy. Boundaries can reveal your fears: your fear of creating conflict or your fear of not being liked. You want to please others and don't want to cause trouble. It can feel scary to tell the truth or say no, which is what you do when you set a boundary.

Before you look at how to set a boundary, it's important to explore your mindset first.

- What makes it hard for you to set boundaries?
- What do you fear might happen?
- What are you afraid you might lose?

Pondering these questions shows you why drawing the line can be hard for you. You may already know, but it's good to be clear on it. Often fears disappear the moment you put them onto paper.

It's also important to get clear on what setting boundaries brings you. So explore that next.

- What's the benefit of setting boundaries?
- What will you gain?
- What do you no longer have to endure when you do?
- How will this make your life better?
- How much energy will this save you?

There's one more thing that helps you set boundaries, and that's being clear on who might oppose them, and why. The only people who object to you having boundaries are people who win something by you *not* having them. Drawing lines doesn't serve their agenda, and they don't like it.

But those aren't the people you want in your life. They don't love or respect you. People who love you respect your boundaries. In fact, having clear boundaries is a gift for people around you! It's crystal clear to them what you do and don't accept. That saves them the hassle of having to guess what you will or won't tolerate. They may not understand your boundaries, but they'll respect them. In general, people respect people with clear boundaries.

So now all it comes down to is setting your boundary and sticking to it. You need to be clear of the consequences of crossing your lines. Lay the ground rules and act accordingly.

It's okay if others don't understand your boundary. They don't have to. It's *your* boundary, not theirs. It's okay if others get angry when you stick to your guns. That's no reason to let them cross the line.

Set your boundaries and inform people about them using clear language. You don't have to apologize, justify, or explain yourself. Simply tell them. And once you have done that, all you have to do is stick to your rules.

Let's say, for example, that your client calls always go over time. Your clients count on your calls taking longer than they paid for. So how do you communicate that this will change? By keeping it simple and clear, like this: "As of now, I honor both your and my time by no longer going over time on our calls. This means that from now on a one-hour call will actually take one hour. This will help us be more focused and make the most of our time. Thank you for your cooperation!"

Next time you talk to your client, implement your new rule. You can do this by announcing you're about to wrap up ten minutes in advance: "We have ten minutes left. What would you like to focus on in that time?" Make sure to STOP when the hour is over! If necessary, tell them you'll pick up where you left off next time. Or you can refer them to another way they can get your support after your call ends: "You can get further support via email / in the Facebook group."

The MOST important part about setting boundaries is for you to completely stand behind them. If you have *any* doubts about your own rules or don't plan on enforcing any consequences when people break them, others *smell* this, and will definitely challenge you! When you're not firm about your own rules, you'll break them—and you'll let others break them—every time.

Reflection

Is there a boundary you can set or stick to?

Divinely Selfish Declarations

* Clear boundaries are a form of self-love and self-care.
* I allow myself to have boundaries and stick to them.
* It's safe for me to have boundaries.
* People who don't respect my boundaries have no place in my life.
* The only people who don't like my boundaries are the ones who benefit from walking all over me—and I don't allow that.

———

*Need more help/advice than this one chapter gave you? Sign up for free book bonuses at www.selfishbookgift.com, and you'll receive a master class that dives deep into practical tips and the mindset needed to set boundaries.

Chapter 44

Take No Shit

Have you seen that meme that says, "Do no harm and take no shit"? I don't know who came up with that, but I wholeheartedly agree! It's wonderful to be loving, compassionate, empathetic, respectful, and kind. And it's normal to accept the same treatment in return! You're no one's doormat or therapeutic punching bag.

Do no harm and take no shit. That really says it all.

Reflection

If you stopped taking any shit, what would be different?

Divinely Selfish Declaration

* I do no harm and take no shit. I'm no one's doormat or therapeutic punching bag!

PART TWO

Questions, Fears, Concerns

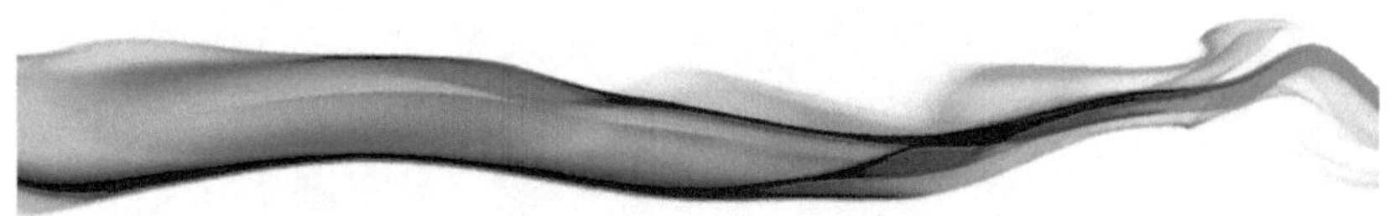

Introduction to Part Two

Putting yourself first can trigger questions and fears. Most of them are already addressed in Part One, but I have separated them out as individual problems in this part of the book to make it easy for you to find your question.

The fears in the following chapters are issues I've heard countless times from the women I have coached over the past two decades. If you recognize anything, know you're not the only one who runs into it!

Anything that might stop you from prioritizing yourself is most likely covered in one of the following chapters. In the unlikely case you don't find your issue *anywhere* in this book, the solution is to focus on what you *gain* by putting yourself first instead of focusing on what you *think* you might lose. To focus on the upsides of letting your soul run your life instead of focusing on what you fear might happen if you do. To give yourself permission to think of yourself more. And to decide not to let others determine your way of living, but to determine that yourself. You're the boss and how you live your life is entirely up to you!

Chapter 1

The Fear You Have to Choose Between Yourself OR Others

Women often fear they have to choose between taking good care of others OR taking good care of themselves. They feel stuck between being selfless OR selfish, between being kind OR being a bitch, between speaking up OR keeping the peace, etc.

At its core, the fear is that you always have to choose between yourself OR others. As if these were mutually exclusive. As if choosing your own well-being and happiness automatically means that others will suffer.

It's not true. You do NOT have to choose. You can prioritize your happiness and still be kind, nurturing, and caring, but not at your own expense. It's not one or the other. That's a fear-based, scarcity-driven, old-world belief based on competition and lack. But that's not how life operates. Follow your soul and do what's genuinely good and nurturing for yourself. This automatically serves the good of the whole because you are part of the whole.

You don't have to choose. Your own self-love and self-care includes others, but not at the cost of depleting yourself. You can be kind and strong, nurturing and fierce, caring and powerful, Divinely Selfish, and full of love and empathy. No one loses when you prioritize yourself.

But when you don't put your needs first and you live for others, it's to your own detriment and EVERYONE loses—especially you.

Reflection

If you fully trusted that you could prioritize your soul, dreams, wants, and needs AND still be there for others, what would change for you?

Divinely Selfish Declarations

* The more I care for myself, the more I can care for others.
* The more I love myself, the more love I have for others.
* The happier I am, the more happiness I can spread around.

Chapter 2

The Fear of Letting Others Down

How can you be Divinely Selfish when others need you? When you have to take care of a sick loved one or a child? Or if, for some other reason, you're in a phase of your life where you don't have a lot of time for yourself? *Can* you prioritize yourself then?

The answer is that yes, you can. You may want more time for yourself than you're able to get. You may have to compromise your own needs here and there. AND . . . you can still set boundaries. You can still find time for yourself, if only five minutes. You can still find ways to fill your own cup even when you're taking care of others. Always look at what IS possible, at what you REALLY have to do, and what you can skip or delegate.

I made a conscious decision not to have children, so I don't have personal experience in juggling caring for others and having enough space for myself. But I've coached countless women on finding time for themselves while also caring for their children and / or parents. Without exception, they've been able to create more time, space, and joy for themselves.

In EVERY situation you can be mindful of what you say *yes* to and what you say *no* to. Be aware of what you are and aren't willing to do or accept. There's always SOMETHING you can do to care for yourself. Maybe that means you put off cleaning your house or let someone else do it instead. Maybe you can lower your expectations of what you think you should do or live up to. Maybe others can do more. Maybe you can say *no* to certain demands or obligations. Maybe you can hand over responsibilities and ask for help. Eventually you'll be able to let go of the guilt or worry about what others think of you.

This all begins with giving yourself permission to find time for yourself. To give yourself permission to lower the bar of what you think being a wonderful mother / wife / partner / daughter / friend should be. To give yourself permission to take care of yourself and take time for yourself, even when others need you. To claim time for yourself to do things you enjoy, and to make it your priority to give this to yourself.

Let go of feeling guilty. Let go of old conditioning that tells you to put others first. Let go of the idea that you're being selfish. Give yourself permission to carve out time for yourself. Once you decide to take more time for you, the opportunities to do so will fall into place.

Reflection

If you carve out time for yourself even when others need you, what would be different?

Divinely Selfish Declarations

* I don't have to sacrifice my well-being for that of another person.
* I can take good care of myself while caring for others.
* I give myself full permission to take time for myself, even when others need me.
* The better care I take of myself, the better I can take care of others.

Chapter 3

The Fear of People Judging You

One thing is certain: people WILL judge you. That's what they do. They have opinions. Some of their judgments are positive, but that's not what you're usually afraid of. No, it's the negative judgments you fear! Because . . .? Let's think about that for a moment. What *exactly* do you fear? How could anyone's opinion of you ever harm you?

I absolutely understand how hurtful comments can be. I'm not a robot or made of stone, and I've definitely been hurt by what other people have said. But what about it was painful, exactly? It was mostly that their comment resonated with a painful opinion I already had about myself . . . THAT'S what hurt the most.

The activation of my doubts was painful. What was also hard was the idea that my contribution wasn't valued, that I wasn't fully seen, that I wasn't fully acknowledged. But . . . this, too, showed me where I wasn't seeing, acknowledging, or valuing myself yet. Because I didn't value myself in some areas, I was more vulnerable to other people's judgments.

Yes, people's opinions and judgments of you can absolutely hurt and trigger pains you'd rather not feel. But that's no reason to stop being true to yourself. The pain of dishonoring yourself and not being true to your soul is more distressing and soul-crushing than anyone's judgment of you could ever be!

The solution to this fear is twofold. The first is to love and accept yourself. The more you accept and love yourself, the less power other people have to hurt you. What about yourself don't you like? What do you think you should change? What do you feel guilty or ashamed about? The answers to these questions will show you which parts of yourself need some extra love and acceptance. The second is to surround yourself with people who love and support you for who you truly are, exactly as you are. When you have a circle of loved ones encouraging you, the opinions of strangers don't matter that much anymore.

People will judge you no matter what you do! Ask yourself, what would you rather be judged for: *not* being true to yourself and *not* doing what you love to do? Or for following your soul and your dreams and being true to yourself? I know what I choose . . . how about you?

Reflection

What would be different if you stopped letting your fear of judgment hold you back?

Divinely Selfish Declarations

* Others will always judge me, no matter what I do. That doesn't stop me from doing what I want and being who I am!
* I don't let anyone's judgment or criticism stop me from doing what I'm called to do.
* I surround myself with people who love me for who I am.

Chapter 4

The Fear of Not Being Liked

Not being liked is a big fear for many women. Not surprisingly, because, as I mentioned before, women are still raised and conditioned to want to be liked. Our likeability has determined our value—and this desire to be liked survives in women today. That's why the need to be liked affects women more than men, even though they can be people-pleasers as well. People rarely complain about men being unlikeable, and even when it does happen, being labeled unlikeable doesn't have any negative consequences on their career. For women, being called unlikeable can impact their career and opportunities.

This conditioned need can turn you into a people-pleaser. There are several ways women are taught to please others: by making themselves look beautiful, by being quiet, by dumbing themselves down, by making men feel more important or giving them control, by trying to be perfect, and by always smiling. Almost all women have been told at least ONCE in their life to smile more or to "Give us a smile, love." NO ONE EVER says that to a man!!!

Shake off those old messages, conditioning, and expectations. You're more powerful than that! Be as kind as you like, but only when it feels good to you. There's nothing wrong with being firm, smart, ambitious, or not looking pretty. So what if someone doesn't like you? Your value is NOT determined by your likeability. Your value is not determined by others AT ALL. You're valuable because you're alive.

You're worthy because you're alive. There can always be people who aren't fond of you. So what? It's not the end of the world. You don't like everyone either, do you?

The most important thing is that YOU like you. Focus on the people who love and like you and forget about those who don't. When someone doesn't like you, this says little to nothing about you! It's just someone's opinion of you. Maybe they don't like you because they're jealous. Who knows? Whatever it is, other people's opinions say *nothing* about you and *everything* about someone else's *idea* of you. That's all it is.

The best you can do is to focus on loving and liking yourself so you'll care a lot less about others not liking you. Focusing on yourself frees you up to be true to yourself and to do what you love.

Reflection

What would be different if you weren't afraid that others won't like you?

Divinely Selfish Declarations

* I enjoy it when others like me, but I don't lose any sleep over it if they don't.
* I don't need others to like me as long as *I* like me.
* It's safe for me to not be liked.
* I'm valuable and worthy because I'm alive—I don't have to earn it by changing who I am or pleasing others.
* I know and like who I am. Other people's opinions about me don't change how I think and feel about myself.

Chapter 5

The Fear of Conflict or Confrontation

Fear of conflict usually stems—like most of our behaviors—from childhood experiences. This fear makes you behave in ways that are more about avoiding clashes than about taking a stand for yourself and speaking (and living) your truth. But you're an adult now. Even if a conflict arises, it's not the end of the world and it won't kill you. (With the occasional exception, of course. If you're in an abusive situation or live with an unpredictable, violent partner, it's a different story, and you need help to get out safely.)

I don't like conflicts either, but I don't back down on things that matter to me. I don't avoid conflicts at all costs. IF a conflict arises, I'll be able to handle it. I was always able to and always will be. Just like you are!!

What's the worst that could happen? Seriously, think about it: what IS the worst that could happen? Are you absolutely certain this WILL happen? And if it did, are you absolutely certain you wouldn't be able to handle it?

Make a list of twenty-five reasons why you would be able to handle a conflict IF one ever arose. I know you have what it takes to deal with it. Making this list will show *you* that, too.

Here are some tips to help you take control of a situation that's headed toward a conflict. In general, it helps to be grounded and breathe deeply when you have a tough conversation or speak your truth. Focus on your breath as that helps you stay calm. Stick to the facts and to your own feelings. Don't blame others and don't tell others how they should feel or what they should do. Set an intention upfront, that can help, too. Write out how you choose to feel before, during, and after the conversation. Listen to the other person. Take responsibility for your part of the situation and let others take their own responsibility.

When you follow these guidelines, you'll be fine. Heck, you'll be fine if you don't follow them, too! You've survived and you've probably handled other conflicts before, so don't let the fear of conflict stop you from taking a stand for yourself.

Reflection

If you were no longer afraid of conflict OR you didn't let the fear of conflict stop you, what would be different?

Divinely Selfish Declarations

* I no longer let my fear of conflicts hold me back or make me change who I am.
* I take a stand for myself and what matters to me, even when this could lead to conflict.
* I can handle anything in my life, including conflict.
* I'm powerful and strong.
* It's safe for me to take a stand and speak my truth.

Chapter 6

The Fear of Being Criticized

What if you get criticized?! This is another fear that can stop you from being true to yourself and doing what you love.

Well, if someone criticizes you, then what? This, too, is not the end of the world. I know receiving criticism can hurt. But fear of hearing it doesn't have to stop you. And you can *learn* how not to let it hold you back any longer. You can do that by first realizing that there are two kinds of criticism: constructive and deconstructive. Constructive criticism is when someone genuinely wants to help you improve something. Deconstructive criticism is when someone tries to find fault with you or the way you've done something. They're looking for a way to blame you or make you feel bad about yourself. It's not meant to help you improve.

The constructive kind may help you. It can still sting, but don't let the fear of the pain rob you of the opportunity to learn from it. Deconstructive criticism you can ignore. It's not helpful and most likely not *intended* to be—it's usually meant to bring you down or show you your place.

I remember an email I received after I wrote my first article in English when I switched from working only in The Netherlands to working globally. A woman wrote that she strongly suggested I hire an editor to check my work, or she feared I would never succeed and would have to close down my business sooner or later. I instantly knew this was not meant as helpful feedback. I could sense she was jealous that I took a giant leap and went for my dream, which made her painfully aware that she was too scared to follow her own dreams. I didn't respond and deleted the email. A while later I wrote a blog about criticism, and how sometimes people mask their attempt to make you feel bad as well-meaning (and usually unsolicited) advice. I mentioned this email in my blog and wrote how I sensed that the advice was driven by jealousy. A couple of days later I received a postcard from the woman who emailed me. She apologized and told me I was right: she *had* felt jealous because I chose to go for my dream and she was too scared to do that herself . . . .

How do you know which feedback to listen to and which to ignore? And how do you deal with the pain or feelings that can come up when faced with a situation like this?

The first thing you need to learn is not to take anything personally. I know, that's easier said than done. It requires a firm foundation of self-acceptance, self-confidence, self-esteem, and self-love. All of these things you can work on and practice. Even after you've built that foundation, you can still feel shaky, offended, or hurt when people criticize you. But it won't completely paralyze or hold you back anymore.

Absolutely nothing is personal. It can FEEL personal, but it never is. Everything anyone says about another person (INCLUDING compliments and praise!) is always and only an expression of *their* beliefs, perspective, story, and perception of you, the world, and others. It can be *aimed* at you, and you can be the subject they talk about, but at its essence, it's NOT about you.

Again, I totally get how it can feel damned personal, even when you know it isn't. I take things personally, too, sometimes, even though I know better. But it doesn't hurt for days or cripple me as much as it used to. And I certainly don't let the idea that someone might not like me or criticize me stop me from doing what's best for myself. You're holding proof of that in your hands right now. ;-)

Remind yourself that nothing is personal. Stop seeing critique as the enemy. Sometimes you can learn from it and use it to your advantage. Explore your thoughts and stories about yourself, your work, etc. What is it you think or believe? Is that *really* true? Is your self-talk constructive or deconstructive? Is it loving or harsh?

When someone else says something negative that resonates with a belief you already have about yourself, it's extra hurtful. Not because of what that person said, but because the pain you already inflict on yourself gets an extra push from something in the outside world. If this pain were not alive in you already, it would hurt a lot less, if at all.

So explore your mindset, your stories, and beliefs. Practice self-love and self-acceptance. Heal what needs healing, shift what needs shifting, do what you can to build your self-esteem and self-confidence.

When you feel good about yourself, what you do, and how you do it, what others think about you won't matter that much anymore. Focus on liking yourself more instead of trying to avoid criticism or conflicts that may never come.

My final tip is to start a compliment journal. In it, you write EVERY compliment, positive review, and testimonial you get. I know, I just told you that praise isn't personal and is not about you, but reading through these kind words can help you build your self-confidence and self-esteem! It creates a loving, protective layer between you and unkindness—in case you need it. All you have to do is read through your compliment journal to shift your mood and heal your wounds.

Reflection

If you didn't let fear of criticism stop you, what would be different?

Divinely Selfish Declarations

* Nothing is personal, and for that reason I take nothing personally.

* My own self-criticism is my worst enemy, not what others may think or say about me.

* I take from feedback that which benefits me and I ignore the rest.

Chapter 7

The Fear of Disapproval

As we grew up, most of us learned that when we were *good* and well behaved, we received compliments and affection. Approval felt good and made us feel loved. If we grew up with an abusive or violent parent, our need for approval became our survival mechanism: approval kept us safe; doing something that wasn't approved of could get us hurt. In either case, as an adult you can still feel a need for validation. You confuse approval with being loved and / or being safe because of your upbringing.

The need for approval is something you can get over, though. Start by asking yourself why you need someone's approval. What does it bring you? What underlying need does it fulfill? What do you fear will happen when someone disapproves of you or what you do?

The answers to why you seek approval are usually something along these lines: You need to feel that you belong. You need to be acknowledged. You need to be seen. You need to feel loved. You need to feel valued. You need to feel safe.

Once you know what it is you TRULY need, look for ways that you can give this to yourself. Where are you not seeing, loving, valuing, or acknowledging yourself? What about yourself do *you* disapprove of? What about yourself can you acknowledge, value, like, and love more?

Give yourself permission to belong and to be who you are. Practice loving and accepting yourself more. Stop feeling reliant on what others think of you and start seeing yourself in a more positive light. Work on your self-confidence and self-esteem by focusing on your strengths instead of your weaknesses. Celebrate and acknowledge your successes and wins. Look at what's right about you instead of what you think is wrong about you. Practice honoring your own truth above everything else and walking your own path instead of another's.

You don't need anyone's approval for anything but your own.

Reflection

If you let go of your need for other people's approval, what would be different?

Divinely Selfish Declarations

* I don't need anyone's approval but my own.
* I don't need anyone's approval to belong or to exist: I belong because I AM.
* I don't need to please others to be seen, acknowledged, or loved.
* I don't need others to see or acknowledge me because I see and acknowledge myself.

Chapter 8

The Fear of Rejection

The fear of rejection is the fear of losing love, or acceptance, or belonging, if you don't live up to other's expectations of you. It's also the fear of being cast out. Thousands of years ago, not being part of a group was dangerous. It was impossible, or at least incredibly hard, to survive outside of or without your community or family.

But those days are gone. Your survival no longer depends on being included by others. And you don't have to worry about ending up all alone in a cold and lonely world. Some people *may* reject you, yes. But those who love you won't reject you.

If the fear of rejection haunts you, the first thing to do is look inward. In what ways are you rejecting yourself? What parts of yourself are you rejecting? Start by embracing, accepting, and even loving these parts of yourself.

If something happens that makes you feel rejected, explore if it's *really* the case. When someone says *no* to your offer, they aren't rejecting you personally, they are only rejecting your offer. When someone doesn't come to your party, they aren't rejecting you, they declined the invitation to your party. Are you *really* being personally rejected? And if so, what do you think that means? It's the meaning you give to the rejection that determines how much it hurts. When your partner leaves you for someone else and you decide this means that you're unlovable and you'll never find another lover, it hurts like hell. When your partner leaves you for someone else and you decide that person is an idiot, it still hurts, but not as much. (And getting over it is easier, too.)

Often, what feels like rejection has nothing to do with you at all. Remember what I wrote in a previous chapter: at its essence, nothing is personal. So take nothing personally, especially when it's related to business. Explore what it is you truly fear about rejection. What do you think you will lose if someone rejects you? What do you think it means? The answers to these questions show you what doubts and beliefs you can heal, shift, or let go of.

Throughout your life people will turn you down, say *no* to your invitations, and opportunities will pass you by. Don't take them personally and don't blow the rejection out of proportion. Yes, it doesn't feel good, and express your emotions when this is the case. Vent, cry, grieve, and feel sad. Get support from others and ask for their help. You'll get through this. I'll repeat something I've shared in other chapters, too: practice more self-love and self-acceptance. Recognize your value and your worth. Find ways to strengthen your self-confidence and self-esteem. Acknowledging your value prevents you from blowing the fear of rejection out of proportion or stopping you. Yes, you may hear *no* if you make someone an offer. But if you never take the risk to be rejected, you won't win much either. Letting go of your fear of rejection will benefit you TREMENDOUSLY in every area of your business and life!

Reflection

If fear of rejection no longer stopped you, what would be different?

Divinely Selfish Declarations

* The more I love and accept myself, the less I fear rejection.
* Even when someone rejects me, this doesn't diminish my value or my worth.
* Rejection isn't personal.
* Rejection isn't the end of the world—it's what *I* think it means that hurts the most.

Chapter 9

The Fear of Looking Selfish

Something I hear quite often is, "But I don't want people to think I'm selfish!" Ehm . . . okay. Why would that be such a terrible thing? Worrying about people thinking you're selfish all goes back to people pleasing, the need for approval, and the need to be liked. Once you stop worrying about what others think, you also stop worrying about others calling you selfish, or whatever you don't want people to think of you.

The first question to ask yourself is what *exactly* is so bad about being called selfish? What *exactly* are you afraid of? Why are you afraid of being judged in this way? What do you think you will lose or miss out on?

Forget about what others think of you or what you *think* they think of you. What's most important is what *you* think of you. The more positive you think about yourself, the less you will care what others think.

As I mentioned before: most people don't think about you at all, or all that much. Everyone thinks about themselves pretty much all the time. Even when they think about something or someone else, they're STILL thinking about themselves: they think about their opinion of the person or situation, how it affects them, or how it makes them feel.

Seriously. Everyone is mostly occupied with themselves, not with you.

Reflection

If you didn't worry about what others think of you or what they might call you, what would be different?

> ### Divinely Selfish Declarations
>
> * I don't worry about what others think of me because I know they don't think about me that much or at all.
> * It doesn't matter what others think of me; it only matters what *I* think of me.
> * The more I love and accept myself, the less I care what others might think about me.

Chapter 10

The Fear of Losing People

Don't be afraid of losing people. You can only lose people who don't truly love or like you. People who genuinely love you don't need you to change who you are; they don't need you to behave in ways that align with their personal agenda.

Yes, you MAY lose people who don't like you standing up for yourself, being true to yourself, and taking good care of yourself. But what kind of people are they? These are the people you don't want in your life to begin with. It's not that you're not good enough for them—it's that they're not good enough for you!

You lose the leeches, abusers, narcissists, and manipulators. You lose the psychopaths and sociopaths. You lose the assholes and the ones who feed on your discomfort and unhappiness. You lose the people who want you to serve their agenda. These are NOT people to hold on to.

True friends and true love NEVER demand you to be someone you're not. True love and true friends want you to be exactly who you are!

The more you are true to who you really are, the easier it will be to attract the people and opportunities that are a perfect match for you. Everything else will (gradually) fall away. That's not something to fear. That's something to celebrate!

Reflection

What would be different when you no longer let your fear of losing people stop you?

Divinely Selfish Declarations

* There is no place in my life for people who don't appreciate me for who I truly am. I'm worth so much more than that!
* I only allow people in my life who love me for who I truly am.
* People who want me to change to suit their agenda or needs can leave now. I don't need them in my life.
* The more I am true to myself, the more I'll attract people into my life who love and respect me for who I truly am.

Chapter 11

The Fear of Disappointing Others

What do you think will happen if you disappoint someone? What do you think you will lose? Start exploring what *exactly* you fear. If you're afraid you'll lose someone's love if you disappoint them, it wasn't genuine love to begin with. When someone only loves you when you do what they want, it's not love. It's manipulation and control.

Remember, you have no control over how someone else feels. How you act is your responsibility, how others receive your actions is their responsibility. You can mean well, do your best, be loving, respectful, and kind . . . and *still* disappoint others.

Make sure you behave in ways that are aligned with your values. Be clear on who you want to be, and how you want to treat others. Own up to it when you make a mistake, correct it, and apologize if needed. Take responsibility for your actions and emotions. Don't put that responsibility on others. Honor your commitments and promises as best you can. Even when you do that, you can still unwillingly or unknowingly disappoint others. But then you also know you did the best you could. That's all you can ever do.

Let go of your fear of disappointing others. No matter what you do or how you do it, it WILL happen! Someone may feel disappointed because you don't love them back. Someone else will be disappointed if you don't want to work with them. Another person will be upset if you don't want to hire them or you don't want to buy from them. People may be disappointed because you can't give them what they ask for or you can't come to their party. But what's the alternative? Should you mold and bend yourself in odd shapes to keep them happy? Should you deny yourself what you need so as not to rock their boat? Should you disappoint or dishonor *yourself* for fear of disappointing them?

No. If you have to choose between disappointing yourself or disappointing another person, choose to honor yourself. True friends can handle the disappointment. Mature adults can handle it. And yes, you need to learn to handle feeling disappointed by others. You can't expect something from others that you're not willing to do yourself.

When you have your own business, you'd better learn to deal with rejection and disappointment. You'll hear *no* a lot and many times you will fail! It's not a big deal. It's part of business and a part of life. It's not personal.

You can handle disappointing others. Others can handle disappointment, too. If they currently aren't handling it well, it's on them to learn to deal with their emotions instead of demanding you to change. Don't worry about disappointing others. Only worry about disappointing yourself.

Reflection

What would be different if you weren't afraid to disappoint others?

Divinely Selfish Declarations

* I'm not worried about disappointing others. My main concern is not to disappoint myself.
* It's safe for me to disappoint others.
* I treat others with kindness, compassion, love, and respect—I treat myself with all of these, too! If my choices disappoint others, that's just the way it is. I'm not changing myself or my decisions to accommodate others.

Chapter 12

Other Fears and Objections

There may be other fears and objections that make it difficult for you to be Divinely Selfish and do what you love. Maybe you fear that you won't be able to make money if you're completely true to your soul. Maybe you're afraid you won't be able to find a partner if you're true to yourself. Maybe you're afraid it's impossible to build your business in complete alignment with your true self.

Whatever it is, the underlying core fears are usually one or more of these:

- The fear that who you are is not good enough.
- The fear that what you do isn't good enough.
- The fear that it's not safe to be who you are.

The solution is always the same: to accept yourself more. To love yourself more.

Explore your underlying needs and see how you can help yourself. Remind yourself of your value and your worth. Work on your self-confidence and self-esteem.

When you do these things, you can still feel fear. But the fear no longer has power over you. It never actually did. Fears are nothing more than a thought in your head and you're fully equipped to deal with them.*

Reflection

If you decided no obstacle or fear could stop you, what would you do?

Divinely Selfish Declarations

* I'm not afraid of my fears. They have no more power over me than I give them.
* My obstacles don't stop me. My desire to be true to myself and my soul is bigger than any obstacle or fear!
* I deeply love, accept, and respect myself. At the very least, I'm in the process of getting there. ;-)
* I live my life on my own terms, in my own way.
* I honor my soul in everything, always.
* I'm a Divinely Selfish Queen, and I love it!

———

*If you need more tools to handle obstacles and fears, check out Book One in the Art of Divine Selfishness Series, *Unmute Your Life - break free from fear & go for what you REALLY want.* In it you'll find lots of different tools and exercises to move through dozens of fears and obstacles. You can find it here: www.unmuteyourlife.com

What's Next?

I hope this book helps you be true to who you are in everything you do. I hope it helps you love, accept, and take care of yourself more. Above all, I hope you put your soul first and follow her lead! I believe that the more people do that, the better off everyone is.

If you're looking for more inspiration or support, I've got you covered.

First, you can get complimentary gifts, which include an in-depth master class on setting boundaries, a permission slip, a collection of reflections, and a collection of Divinely Selfish Declarations here: www.selfishbookgift.com

If you'd like to take a deeper dive into what you learned in this book, check out my online program The Art of Divine Selfishness here: www.divinelyselfishprogram.com

If you're looking for custom support, my private coaching might be perfect for you: www.workwithb.com

And come say, "Hi!" on social media! You can find me here:

Instagram: www.instagram.com/brigitte_van_tuijl/
Facebook: www.facebook.com/brigittevantuijl.artofdivineselfishness/
Twitter: www.twitter.com/brigittevanT

Thank you for reading and playing with this book. I hope you enjoyed it and if so, please leave me a brilliant review! Or just a nice one. That'll make me happy, too. :-)

For now, I wish you all the best, and enjoy becoming a Divinely Selfish Queen!

Love,

Brigitte

Other Books by Brigitte

The Gap - bridge the space between where you are and where you want to be
No matter how big your dream or goal is, realizing it can be easier than you think. This book shows you how.

The Art of Divine Selfishness Series

Book One: *Unmute Your Life - break free from fear & go for what you REALLY want*
This book helps you uncover your TRUE dreams and make them real.

Books in Dutch

Ontdek wat je écht wilt en maak daar (je) werk van
Een praktisch en inspirerend werkboek om zelfstandig in kaart te brengen wat je écht wilt – en daar je werk van te maken.

You can find more information on these books and new books I'm working on at www.booksbybrigitte.com